Decluttering Your Home

Your Simple, Step-by-Step Guide to Declutter Your Home and Live a Clean, Healthy, and Minimalist Life

By Abbey Lincoln

Table of Contents

Introduction iv

Chapter 1 Defining Decluttering 1

Chapter 2 The Ways That Decluttering Benefits Your Home and Your Life 3

Chapter 3 Habits That Lead to Clutter and How to Break Up with Them 5

Chapter 4 The Necessity of Having a Cleaning Routine 10

Chapter 5 How Sentiments Work Against Decluttering 12

Chapter 6 Strategy 1: Decluttering Room by Room 15

Chapter 7 Strategy 2: The Big Purge 54

Chapter 8 Room-by-Room Decluttering vs. One Big Purge 62

Chapter 9 Putting Your Priorities in Perspective 63

Chapter 10 Frequently Asked Questions You Need to Address 69

Conclusion 71

Introduction

This book contains everything you need to start decluttering your home so that you and your family are able to live healthy and happy in a clean and organized environment—free from the burden of looking after too many belongings that are actually crowding your life.

With the help of this book, you can avoid feeling overwhelmed by the mess, be it in the form of trash, bargain, or aspirational clutter. It will allow you to understand that your home is where you should be able to relax and breathe easily, not a place where you find yourself constantly feeling stressed, disoriented, unclean, and emotional because of all the clutter around you.

Simply put, by reading this book and following the tips outlined in it, you will finally feel empowered—in control, productive, and contented in your very own living space.

Chapter 1
Defining Decluttering

Decluttering refers to the process of making decisions about the items you have in your home, whether they belong in your space, serve a purpose, and bring you happiness or move your soul in ways that no words could describe. Decluttering also involves figuring out where each item in your home should belong and taking steps to ensure it is where it should be.

Decluttering is the solution to the presence of clutter in your home and life that comes in different forms:

Trash clutter
This includes items that you can easily do without, but are instead masquerading as clutter in different parts of your house. The things included in this type of clutter are the easiest to ditch, although they are also the easiest to pile up. Examples of trash clutter are unread newspapers, expired food, unopened magazines, and unsorted mail.

Abundance clutter
Abundance clutter refers to the large number or amount of things you have around your home that never really get used. Stocking up on décor, clothing, and food, among other things, may be your favorite thing to do, especially on weekends. You probably purchase different things in multiples for fear that you would need the exact thing in the future and you cannot imagine yourself without it. But, your preference will change so much that it will be difficult for you to foretell how you would want to dress up or what you would want to eat months or years from now.

Clutter due to lack of storage space
This type of clutter refers to the stuff in your home that isn't actually clutter, but are things that do not have a specific storage space. It can include mail that has not been opened yet, books you have not arranged on the bookshelf, or the cans of unused paint scattered in your garage's corner. Clutter that results from your stuff not having a home will need extra time and steps to handle, since you have to find spaces to store them in before you could start putting them away.

Aspirational clutter
Aspirational clutter includes stuff you purchase in order to gain other people's admiration and respect. Perhaps you buy plenty of gear for a particular hobby that you do not even actively participate in. Maybe you own tons of designer clothes that do not even reflect who you are and what your lifestyle is. Or maybe, you own the latest kitchen appliances when you do not even have an interest in cooking something other than fried eggs. To put it simply, you acquire

aspirational clutter because they say something about you to other people, and not because they add value to your life or because you simply love them.

Bargain clutter

Bargain clutter refers to stuff you accumulate from your weakness for discounts, sales, and gift-with-purchase offers. You find those tiny bottles of shower gel and shampoo in hotel rooms so irresistible that you bring them home without thinking about it. You may find yourself happily surprised that you bought items that were not on your list of things to buy. Bargain clutter results from buying something just because it seems like such a good bargain, even if it ends up never being used.

Sentimental clutter

This type of clutter has to be the most problematic clutter to deal with. Sentimental clutter makes you feel as though you have betrayed the people you love, as well as the special memories of experiences you once shared with them just because you decided to part with it. The problem with sentimental clutter is that it is tied to feelings or emotions, making it almost impossible to give up certain things you own.

Chapter 2
The Ways That Decluttering Benefits Your Home and Your Life

Decluttering allows you to enjoy the following benefits:

You identify the important things in your life
Because decluttering forces you to carefully choose the items to keep around you, you start being more careful with your choices in other aspects of your life as well. For example, you begin deciding that sitting through an entire movie you never wanted to watch in the first place isn't worth it. Or, you no longer see the point of talking nonstop with people who bring toxicity into your day. You might also decide to quit reading books on topics that you do not really care about.

You gain freedom
Clutter has the power to hold you back in case you suddenly want or need to move to another place, especially if simply getting out of the house requires you to step over clothes strewn about on the floor. Having more personal belongings to deal with only makes it more difficult for you to figure out your expenses and logistics when relocating. The truth is that the allure of hobos and nomads has nothing to do with hopping in and out of a moving train or running out of food, but with the ease with which they could pack up their things to go someplace better. And, even if you are not planning to move anytime soon, realize that having less stuff gives you the freedom to redecorate your house or rearrange all rooms as often as you need to. You could easily switch things up to give your surroundings a fresh new look that makes it seem like you did move to a new place.

You find more time for getting things done
Because you're no longer weighed down by the mess in the kitchen, you gain more time to cook great-tasting meals for your family. The fact that you no longer need to spend thirty minutes looking for your car key or trying on clothes to wear to work means you are also saving a huge chunk of your time. Do not be surprised if you get to save about one hour a day, each day, after a deep decluttering project.

You are empowered to address personal issues
Digging through all that clutter will likely have you unearthing plenty of negative memories. It can feel truly liberating to actually get rid the things that remind you of unrealized dreams or sad memories. Plus, you get to create new spaces for items that bring inspiration and happiness to your life.

You begin taking positive risks

Letting clutter rule your life usually means you have lots of unfinished business sitting in your life's back burner. Decluttering allows you to do away with your issues in the past and steers you toward taking bigger risks that help improve your life.

You gain more space

Clearing away all that clutter from your life gives you more space for working, thinking, or simply taking a break. Clutter does have a way of sometimes annoying you at the mere sight of them or physically getting in your way. But, there are also times when clutter crowds your mental space. You find yourself having a hard time focusing on a task because you see the pile of papers sitting on top of the dining table. You may also find it difficult to finish a house chore simply because you know that a huge mess is waiting for you in the next room.

You start understanding yourself better

Holding on to every single item you have ever owned can lead you to believe that you need all of them in your life. But the truth is, getting rid of clutter can help you realize what you truly want in different areas in your life, like your décor and clothes. Eliminating clutter leaves you a home adorned with carefully chosen deco and a minimalist wardrobe that creates maximum impact.

You get to save (and earn) money

It's easy to see that buying less means you also spend less. But then, it can still cost you to clear out all the stuff you acquired at no cost, including your kids' forgotten party favors and your own accumulated freebies. Remember, the cost of each thing you own not only refers to its sticker price, but also includes the cost of having to maintain it as well as to transport it you are moving. Besides saving you money, decluttering can also help you make extra money off your used books, old clothes, and other unwanted and unneeded possessions. And, if you need to sell your house, know that a decluttered home is easier to sell than a messy one.

You find it much easier to clean around the house

To live in a clutter-free home is great, but it takes a lot of your effort and time to clean your home and make sure it stays clean. This is where decluttering is truly a godsend—when you have less clutter to deal with, you no longer have to spend so much time and energy cleaning up everything. This leaves you with more time in your hands to work on other important things or take that much-needed staycation.

You get to break a bad habit

Getting rid of all that clutter in your home and in your life can results in two things: It removes all the items that trigger your bad habits, or it enables you to adopt better ones. For instance, eliminating store-bought cookies from the pantry helps you avoid your usual afternoon binge fest.

Chapter 3
Habits That Lead to Clutter and How to Break Up with Them

Maintaining a mess-free home is no joke, especially if you tend to do the following out of habit:

Not giving every item its own place
Having too many belongings with nowhere to go in your home only leads to clutter that later on becomes difficult to clean up.

Not setting up a cleaning protocol
When you do not have an effective cleaning system in your home, it becomes harder to make sure your belongings are organized and properly maintained. Not following a cleaning schedule also makes it easy for dirt to accumulate underneath chairs and tables, and for used plates and pots to pile up in the sink.

Thinking cleaning is such a chore
Cleaning is a chore that actually becomes enjoyable once you pair it with listening to your favorite music. And, if it's your thing, nothing beats working up a good sweat through dancing to an upbeat song while mopping up floors.

Not figuring out different ways to make space
This bad habit can have you end up living with piles of stuff in every corner and on every surface of your home.

Failing to clean on the go
When you do not follow a cleaning routine, such as folding the blankets every morning, rearranging the throw pillows after each time the kids are done playing with them, and hanging up your clothes every time you came off from work, you should not be surprised if your home ends up looking like a storm went through it.

Not delegating tasks to others
Except when you are living alone, the clutter in your home is always the result of the collective effort of different members. This is the reason cleaning around the house should also be a task that everyone participates in. It would be difficult to keep your house clean if you fail to delegate sweeping, dusting, emptying the trash, and other chores to others.

Failing to keep flat surfaces in your house clear
The need to put something on every surface at home means your countertops are likely hiding

beneath piles of junk mail, your overflowing drawers are probably difficult to open, and you will surely end up living in a less visually appealing and impossible-to-clean house.

Not being smart with storage
Suffering from this habit robs you of the joy of having every possession you have–from cosmetics and jewelry to digital gadgets and kitchen appliances–laid out, clearly seen, and easily accessed.

Not thinking clean
If you truly want to live in a clutter-free environment, then thinking clean should be the first thing in your mind once you step inside your home. This could mean leaving your shoes at the door because you would not want soil and toxins to enter the house where you and your family relax, eat, and sleep.

Breaking Up With Your Bad Habits

It took you some time to develop your bad habits, so you cannot expect your journey in kicking bad behavior to the curb to be painless. But it can be done, if you follow these tips:

Determine your clutter-conducive habits
It isn't enough to acknowledge the fact that you have a bad habit. You truly need to figure out the specific behaviors that you want to change. Start by deciding to change those exact bad habits that you can easily do something about, such as:

Giving up eating on the couch to have your meal at the dining table instead
Rather than nagging your spouse like you always do, send him or her a complimentary text every day

Instead of taking off your shoes in the living room and just leaving them there, put them in the shoe closet

To really get the break-those-bad-habits mood going, you have to be able to pinpoint the exact things you need to be working on.

Learn your clutter triggers
For you to be able to conquer all of your bad habits, you have to realize that the manner in which you make decisions is a big factor. People tend to keep on practicing bad behaviors without having an idea that they are actually doing them. Remember that every bad habit is the result of five cues, namely time, location, emotional state, immediately preceding action, and other people. Familiarizing yourself with these cues will help you understand the root causes of those bad habits. Whenever you catch yourself creating clutter by dropping your keys and loose change on the dining table after work, immediately take note of the following:

When is it taking place? (4:30 pm)
Where are you? (at home, in the dining room)
How are you feeling? (tired to the bone)
What were you doing before this? (driving home from the office)
Who is with you at the moment? (nobody)

Doing this for several days can help you figure out whatever is triggering your keys-cluttering habit, which, in this case, is you feeling so tired after getting off from work.

Mull it over first
It helps to spend thirty days pondering on your bad habit prior to doing something to change it. Although you're hankering to eliminate a specific bad behavior in this instant, it is important for you to first write down all the reasons you want to get rid of it. Then, for an entire month, take note of each time you find yourself doing the bad habit. Preparing yourself this way leaves you engaged in habit-conquering mode and feeling confident that you can nip any bad habit in the bud.

Take baby steps
Adopting a new, better habit is a task that takes a lot of effort and time, but eliminating a bad one can be even more difficult. This is why you have to have a lot of patience with yourself. Rather than making major transformations, strive to concentrate on one behavior at a time. Also, take the smallest steps possible to get you from acknowledging a bad habit and actually changing it for the better or replacing it with a new one. With your tendency to wait for clothes to pile up before doing the laundry, for instance, a small improvement such as washing clothes once they take up half of the hamper makes a huge impact in the end, even encouraging you to add other small improvements.

Switch up your environment
Later on, you may notice that doing the same bad habits in the same location can cause your surroundings to become your trigger. For example, the office's parking lot can turn into your cue for smoking if you usually go on a smoke break in that place. It truly helps to change your environment in any way you can, especially if you apply the 20-second rule along with it, which is to make sure it takes you twenty seconds longer to begin doing a bad habit. An example would be to transfer all junk food behind the pantry to make it harder for you to get to them, and then to put healthy alternatives in front. This is a case in which you are pretty much counting on your laziness, eating the food that you can grab at faster.

Expect and prepare for setbacks
It would be wise to review your progress (or lack thereof) in changing your bad habits from time to time, especially when you catch yourself committing a relapse on a bad day. Having a setback is okay, so it is best for you to expect it to happen. The important thing is that you have prepared a plan for getting yourself back on track, then using the experience as a means of identifying what took place and the ways you could prevent it from happening again.

Change your mindset about your clutter-inducing ways

Admit it or not, although you hate a particular bad behavior, such as biting your nails or littering your kitchen countertop with paperwork, you generally keep doing it for the simple reason that it gives you some sense of satisfaction. Whenever you catch yourself feeling great about a bad behavior, do your best to reframe it by reminding yourself of all the negativity it brings to your life. This is one of those times when becoming a hater is actually a positive thing.

Make yourself pay for your bad cluttering habits

Force yourself to feel really bad about doing a bad habit to increase your chances of completely getting rid of it. An effective motivator is money, so try:

Going the "swear jar" route

Giving family and friends a dollar for each time you are caught doing a bad behavior

Rewarding yourself with a new outfit at the end of the month after not giving in to your bad habit each day

Getting the 21Habit app, which gives you a reward or a penalty (a dollar per day) for twenty-one days of beating or giving in to a bad behavior

Set up reminders

Even if you start out intending to break your bad habits for good, you can't help but do them when your willpower weakens. For instance, you may commit to buying just one outfit every three months to help reduce clutter in your home, but then you break that commitment the moment you pass by a clothing store's display window while you're feeling blah. This is why it helps to set up reminders for yourself for those down-in-the-dumps moments.

Search for better reasons for quitting your bad cluttering habits

You may fully understand that it is not a good thing to eat fast food on a daily basis or to exercise only once a week, but that knowledge may not be adequate for you to kick your bad behavior to the curb. You may find that when replacing a specific bad habit with a better behavior, doing the latter does not give you the same psychological or emotional satisfaction that the bad habit provides. Therefore, on top of realizing that you need to stop consuming fast food every day to avoid health problems, you can be more effective at encouraging yourself to quit the bad habit because doing so helps you achieve the lean and toned body you have been working on for the past six months.

Be kind to yourself

This is especially important if getting rid of a bad habit does not happen right away. You already know that changing a bad habit is not an overnight task, which is why there is no use beating yourself up for not seeing any progress for a while. The fact is, your brain takes a while to develop new thinking patterns and for new behaviors to get into action.

Out with it

Broadcasting your bad habit to everyone may actually be a good thing. It may also be discomforting, but letting everyone know about your bad behavior can strongly motivate you to give it up since you would not want to be told all the time that you need to quit it.

Chapter 4
The Necessity of Having a Cleaning Routine

Sticking to a cleaning routine allows you to live a less stressed, happier, more comfortable, and rewarding life for the following reasons:

You avoid wasting your time
Although this sounds too simplistic, spending several minutes to clear away items the moment you are finished using them is an effective way of taming clutter in your home. This strategy will leave you with less mess to clean up after, as well as help you search for an item you need to use almost instantly.

You gain more control
Whenever you feel as though your life is out of control, it helps to look around the house and observe its true state. It may be littered with toys and crumbs or it may be decorated with stains, all of which can cause you to feel frustrated and anxious. The truth is, you can reclaim your power over your possessions and your home with the aid of a cleaning routine. You will find that simply wiping down surfaces, sweeping crumbs off the floors, and storing items when not in use can immediately uplift your spirits. Committing yourself to a cleaning schedule takes a lot of time and effort, but the payoff is worth it.

You have fewer repairs and maintenance to deal with
When you see to it that your appliances in the home are kept in good condition, you enjoy the benefit of spending less money on replacing or repairing them. And, the way to accomplish this is to make sure to clean them. It may not seem much, but giving your dishwasher, washing machine, and other appliances a bit of extra care and attention ensures that they will keep on functioning smoothly and that you can avoid unnecessary expenses in the long run. You may have second thoughts about finding the time to do all that maintenance work, but regularly following a cleaning schedule can help you easily achieve this.

You get a sense of accomplishment
Crossing something off your list of things to do, like cleaning and decluttering the bathroom, provides such a big boost in energy, happiness, and self-satisfaction that you cannot help but be motivated to keep on following your cleaning routine for many years to come.

You become more productive
When you really think about it, it's hard to get your creative juices flowing if you are surrounded by clutter. Even just functioning is nearly impossible to do when you find grime and dirt

everywhere you look. When you strive to keep your home clean, you are also giving yourself a clear mental space to focus on and accomplish the tasks you have to do.

You feel less guilty over taking things easy

You may have caught yourself feeling guilty because you are reading a book or watching videos. It is difficult to take a break when you are constantly thinking of the thirty-one important things you need to be doing, which includes cleaning your home. This is where a cleaning schedule comes in handy. You can spread out your cleaning activities all through the week, then pencil in a time for relaxation once you are done for the day. This way, you feel like you have earned your right to take some downtime and you no longer have to feel so guilty doing it.

You get inspired to do more

Vacuuming floors, scrubbing down the bathroom tiles, and doing other cleaning tasks can get your heart pumping and your muscles flexing, so much so that it almost feels like you are working out at the gym. If you do not have a gym membership or the will to exercise, but you'd really want to get healthy, fit, and active, you could just take on the list of things to do in your cleaning schedule. In as little as a few minutes, you will have worked up a good sweat in the comfort of your home and at no cost. Who knew doing the laundry is the same as doing cardio?

You create opportunities to be more hospitable

When you live with clutter in your home, it is hard not to be embarrassed about it in front of friends. You could end up explaining too much, without even being asked, about the state of your house because you worry that how your home looks like is a reflection of how you are as a person. But, you do not need to clean your house so that it impresses the people who might drop by. Sometimes, something as simple as clearing away the clutter on surfaces for an entire fifteen minutes, then putting the removed items back to where they should be is all it takes to create a tidy atmosphere around the house.

You have a healthier family

Clutter attracts dust, dander, mold, and bacteria that can give you and your family asthma, allergies, and other health issues. When you make sure to follow a regular cleaning schedule, you reduce the likelihood that your family gets sick and increase your chances of living healthy and happy.

Chapter 5
How Sentiments Work Against Decluttering

Sentiments make it harder for you to let go of certain things in your life. As a result, decluttering your home becomes a more difficult task. Deciding what to keep and what to give up becomes a real struggle when you have to deal with the following emotions:

You feel as though you are committing a betrayal against a family member or the wonderful memories you have of him or her.

You find it difficult to let go of things that have a romantic value, including your wedding dress that you wore once and will surely never wear again.

You could almost cry thinking about parting with your boxes of birthday cards and wedding/bridal shower/baby shower invitations, even if you have not even looked through them for more than a year.

You feel more than a bit uneasy about donating your hole-y high school sweatshirt or the pair of special occasion heels that no longer fit comfortably.

You think you are being disrespectful to a specific era of your life if you pass on your teenage son's baby blankets to his baby cousin

Dealing With Items That Mean Much to You

The bad news is that you almost feel like your heart is being ripped out just by thinking about parting with items that have sentimental value. The good news, however, is that there are ways for you to cope with your sense of loss.

Let go of the guilt

The truth is that people usually keep sentimental items out of guilt, not because of feelings of nostalgia or love. Unless the cause of your guilt is because you stole something, cheated, or lied, guilt is a completely unhelpful emotion that you should be having no business with. Never allow yourself to indulge in guilty feelings whenever you're deciding what to do with your sentimental clutter. Even if you have a valid reason for feeling bad about a relationship or experience, know that keeping your great grandmother's monstrous-looking figurine will not be able to remedy it.

Avoid turning gifts into burdens

People usually keep gifts because they believe that the family and friends who gave them the items will surely expect these to be on display in their homes. The truth is, a giver may not be expecting his or her gift to be flaunted to others. You should also realize that what you do with a gift you receive is your decision alone.

Figure out whether an item is worth keeping

Make sure to ask yourself whenever you are evaluating sentimental clutter exactly what you are feeling sentimental about. More often than not, what you value is not the item itself but the memories of a person, time, or place you associate with it. Know that you can still keep those memories without having the physical reminder staring you in the face every day of your life.

Virtually preserve your memories

When handling photographs or documents that have sentimental value, especially when you really have no need of the original copies, you could consider scanning and saving them instead of putting them away in boxes. You can also choose to virtually preserve children's toys, a beautiful lamp, an antique chair, and other three-dimensional objects by taking photos of them.

Donate special items to local organizations

Instead of feeling obligated to treat a collection of photos and documents previously owned by a loved one who recently died with special respect, think about the value it has in a local history or archive museum's point of view. Just avoid dumping your sentimental clutter on unsuspecting organizations; instead, do your research first to know if they will welcome the thought of receiving those items.

Pass your heirlooms on to relatives

Your unwanted family heirlooms and other stored-for-ages-and-collecting-dust inherited objects may be your relatives' treasures. So, instead of getting rid of these items right away, ask whether they would want to have the heirlooms for themselves.

Repurpose unusable items

You can still retain an unusable object's sentimental value without it cluttering your home and your life by creating something new out of it. You can remove a precious stone from an old-fashioned ring and re-set it into a modern, stylish band, or you can transform a unique-looking board from a rather bulky dresser into an elegant floating shelf.

Pick one and let go of the rest

You probably inherited a collection of fake fruits from your mother, who inherited it from your grandmother, and now you are stuck with it and have no idea how to let go of it without feeling guilty. What you can do is to keep a single fruit from the group to represent the memories or sentiments behind it.

Find them a new home

In case you feel undecided about getting rid of a sentimental object or stowing it in your attic for years to come, keep in mind that you have the option to donate the item to a person who truly needs it. You may have a close friend who appreciates the functional value of that item and will surely put it to good use, and you can rest assured that it will be taken care of.

Give yourself your own baby book

But, you do not have to spend a lot of money in purchasing various craft supplies and tools for scrapbooking. You can simply make do with a glue stick, an unlined notebook, and heaps of creativity. Glue onto the notebook your pictures, special notes, and other bits and pieces, and you will end up having a convenient and clutter-free space to hold your memories.

Chapter 6
Strategy 1: Decluttering Room by Room

Lash Out at Clutter in the Living Room

Relaxing is that one thing that everyone in your family surely wants to do in the living room. But, this is also the space where things like toys, magazines, blankets, and wires go haywire and so it ends up looking too cluttered for comfort. Thankfully, you can follow the decluttering tips below to help you and your family achieve living room bliss.

Keep clutter off flat surfaces

Flat surfaces around your house tend to attract books, magazines, and sheets of paper, and this is especially true with the living room. Family members need a hub for household information, and the living room is usually the most convenient place for this purpose. This is the reason the living room is almost always the most cluttered part of a house. To combat clutter in this space, consider buying a bin, a two-drawer lateral file, or a stackable document cart to put all your papers in. Make the commitment to sort and purge through the files as needed, and make sure other family members do the same.

Display pictures in creative ways

If you have plenty of small picture frames gathered (and causing clutter) in your living room, you can do your decluttering magic by simply finding new ways to display your photos. You can make use of collage photo frames and photo albums to organize and store hundreds of images all at once, and you may find digital photo frames convenient if you never take pictures using film anymore. As for putting your pictures on display, you can do away with using side tables or the mantel and use a wall's vertical space instead. If you love making scrapbooks, you could organize your pictures by occasion or by date, place them in photo boxes, and keep them on your bookshelf's central location.

Make use of your coffee table

Evaluate how you can take advantage of your coffee table's capacity for organizing things instead of relegating it the task of hiding beneath clutter. Your life would be easier (and the clutter in your living room can be reduced) if you can transform your coffee table into a storage container for your remotes, drink coasters, and magazines. Otherwise, you can always add rolling baskets, bins, or low storage cubes under your coffee table.

Establish a game hub

A game cabinet that holds cards and board games would be perfect for your home if you and your family love to play together. While games generally find their way in the TV shelf, it would be convenient to set up a specific place in your living room for them, which could be a separate shelf, a plastic bin under the sofa, or a bookcase. Doing so will not only minimize clutter, but it gives you additional space for storing other items in the living room. If your gaming hub includes a desktop computer, you might do away with a computer armoire and opt to place it in a desk equipped with separate surfaces for the monitor, for doing work, and for paper storage instead.

Get your collectibles under control

When they are not properly organized and stored, collections can quickly take up space in your living room. If you have large collections, you can best display them by showing 3 to 5 pieces at a time and rotating them so that your décor always looks fresh. You can then store the pieces that are not on display in the hall closet.

Put your houseplants in order

Houseplants also have a tendency to cause so much clutter in the living room if you let them be. Make sure they are organized by placing them in decorative pots or in a charming plant stand. How you place each houseplant in the living room depends on what type it is, so remember that when deciding on a plant stand, which usually come in tiered, pedestal, and corner configurations.

Look behind the sofa

The space behind your sofa can be a good place for organizing your extra candles, pillows, and blankets. It is also the perfect spot for placing a low bookcase, cabinet, or trunk, as well as providing a surface for putting your lamp or for displaying a few treasured keepsakes.

Tame those wires

Prevent visual clutter from invading your living room by making sure your wires are not entangled in a giant hot mess. Manage your cords and cables wisely by:

Selecting furniture that can conceal those wires if you would rather not feed them into a wall

Using an area rug to cover up some of the cords around the room

Keeping the wires in a storage container that complements your décor

Using cables and cords of adequate length so you never have to worry about tying up ten feet's worth of wire

Say hello to the wastebasket

If your living room tends to attract trash, consider placing a wastebasket in it. You can avoid having it appear unsightly and smell bad by picking one that complements or matches the décor in the room. Make sure you choose a wastebasket that has a lid and to line it inside using a deodorizing trash bag if food will also be thrown in it.

Be creative with storing your kids' toys

Having kids in the home makes it inevitable for their playthings to get transported from the bedrooms and the playroom into your living room. But, toys can easily turn the room into one that looks like a preschool area, so it is important to invest in smart storage containers. Consider using furniture that can serve the double purpose of adding to the appeal of the living room and serving as storage. This means you can then store toys inside an ottoman (pick one that comes with a lid) or a coffee table (one that has a hinged top would be great) while it still functions as a place for sitting on or for setting beverages. Other practical but still chic toy storage solutions include the following:

Armoire: It is amazing how an armoire can easily house a big collection of toys, especially the bulky ones (baskets and bins can take care of the smaller toys). To ensure your kids have easy access to the toys they frequently play with, place them on the armoire's bottom shelf. You can just close the door of the armoire if you no longer want to see them. Make use of the top surface by displaying some of your personal accessories on it.

Bookcase: Besides making sure your precious first editions are safely tucked away, your bookcase can also serve as a storage container of your kids' most frequently used toys by filling its lower shelves with nice-looking baskets or bins. If preferred, you could add a hanging curtain panel on the bookshelf, which you can then pull to close whenever the toys are not being used by the kids.

Media center: The media center (an open storage, a collection of drawers, or a cabinet) below the TV set can serve as a valuable space for putting away small toys, family movies, and game controllers.

Stylish containers: No one can stop you from adding a grown-up spin on your kids' toy storage containers, so feel free to use your vintage suitcases, metal buckets, and woven baskets.

Wheeled storage: A wagon or a rolling crate will help you quickly grab and hide several toys at once whenever you have unexpected visitors coming by.

Bench: The built-in or freestanding bench you have in the living room can easily function both as a seating area and as a storage solution. Simply stash small toys (placed in bins), games, and puzzles in the space underneath it.

Dresser: If you have an unused but still functional dresser, consider placing it in your living room to hold toys. Action figures, mini cars, board games, puzzles, and other small and flat items can easily go inside the drawers.

Closet: Check out your living room's layout and you may discover an unused space that can function as a walk-in storage solution for your kids' toys. Just pull a curtain over the space when you have guests coming by.

Trunk: While attractive chests and vintage trunks are generally used for storing precious travel souvenirs, linens, and quilts, they are also useful for hiding your kids' colorful dress-up clothes and massive stuffed animals.

Edit your media items

Avoid turning your collection of CDs and DVDs into powerful dust magnets by following these steps in decluttering them:

Turn digital as much as possible to save lots of space. You can simply upload your music onto a cloud. Saving them in physical drives is, of course, another option. If you're worried about relying solely on one backup solution, you could always use both—though completing such a task might require a lot time.

Try combining your collections of original CDs, liner notes, and cover art inside soft case binders that you can browse through flipbook-style; just sort your collections based on genre, artist, or in chronological order. You can take your DVDs and video games out of their packaging before placing them in the binders. You might also want to help a local school or library replace their broken CD cases by donating your own.

Figure out where you would store your edited media collection. It helps to keep them near where you are going to use them, so you might store your video game collection right along with the console and controller. You do not even have to go out and buy fancy bins, shelving, and racks; what's important is that every item is in its place.

Eliminate clutter that do not even belong in the living room

Begin by taking these items out and bringing them back to where they should be:

Endless cushions: Having plenty of cushions in the couch would look nice, but it would also be bothersome to have to move all of them out of the way so you could finally sit down.

Too big or too much furniture: Your home life would be more clutter-free if you choose to have streamlined, smaller furniture, fold-out desks, sliding doors, and ottoman coffee tables.

Beanbags: Beanbags are notorious for being too bulky, taking up way too much space in the living room, not to mention looking out of place with their "for students" vibe. It also only takes a short while for them to look tired and spring a leak, causing major clutter with those tiny polystyrene balls. When it comes to choosing furniture for the living room, it is best to go with square-shaped ones and transfer beanbags to the basement, playroom, or your kids' bedrooms instead.

Stacks of paperwork: Having piles of paperwork in the living room reminds you of unfinished business and prevents you from being able to relax instead. Consider setting up a paperwork station in the hallway so that all incoming mail, files to scan, and other documents are kept for sorting through later, instead of having them end up in your living room.

Exercise equipment: Watching TV while working out may be a good way for you to avoid getting bored with exercise, but then having your cross trainer, rowing machine, or treadmill parked in the living room means you and your family will forever be looking at an eyesore. If the living room is your only option for exercising indoors, try running outside instead.

Too many items on display: A cluttered tabletop or shelf just makes things more difficult to clean.

Magazine rack: Out-of-date magazine issues rarely get read and always end up gathering dust.

Laundry: Piles of laundry are the same as piles of paperwork in that their only purpose for being there in the living room is to remind you that you have a lot of other things on your plate.

Make Clutter Dash Out of Your Dining Room

Because the dining room is where you and your family converge to enjoy each other's company as you share a great-tasting meal and some wonderful conversation, it is important that you keep it as clutter-free as possible. And with that, here are the best decluttering tips on creating a more inviting atmosphere in your dining room:

Get your dining table back

Your dining table does not only give you a place to eat; it's also the space you use to prepare meals, the surface your kids use to do their homework, and the spot your spouse hangs out in while reading. All of that means clutter is inevitable, so here are some tips you can follow to keep your dining table clear for eating:

Have coat and bag hooks installed by your main entrance. This way, your coats, bags, briefcases, and hats stay near the main entrance instead of migrating to the dining table.

Set up a mail processing area by your main entrance. Everything you need to do in handling the mail–from sorting and shredding to recycling and putting in the trash–should take place here, so that the mail never finds its way to the dining table.

Make sure to set your dining table with silverware, cups, and plates as the first meal preparation step. This way, other family members will immediately realize that there is nothing they can do at the dining table other than to eat the meal you have prepared.

See to it that your sideboard or buffet is organized to serve their purpose in the room. What usually happens is that people hardly use their buffets and sideboards because it is cluttered with rarely-used silver service and china. If you really need to have your special event items around, see to it that they are stored in the kitchen cupboards or another more remote place.

Keep any catch-all container, which could be a bamboo platter, a circular rotating tray, or a decorative plate, away from the dining table. It is also so easy for a device made for holding small items like sugar, salt, pepper, condiments, and napkins to hold other items and create clutter, especially when it stays in the dining table after each meal. It's best to place this service in the kitchen when you and your family are not eating.

Have a trash can parked near the dining table. You can hide it in the side table or buffet.

Store your table linens creatively

Avoid making a mess with your tablecloth, napkins, and placemats by following these smart storage ideas:

Towel rod: You could attach several towel rods to one of the basement's walls, behind a closet door, inside the kitchen cabinet, or inside the pantry to make hanging your linens a lot easier.

Wine rack: Those crisscross-patterned cubbies that hold your wine bottles are perfect for holding placements and napkins as well. Just roll up and corral sets together.

Bench (hinge-top): Place a storage bench inside the dining room so that you have a convenient place not just for sitting, but for stashing your napkins and tablecloths as well.

Vintage pie safe/armoire: Aside from adding a pretty touch to your dining room, this furnishing can serve as your portable linen closet.

Old dresser: Repurpose an outgrown dresser into a storage solution for your linens. Place napkins, napkin trivets and rings, and placemats inside the smaller drawers. Fill the larger drawers with folded tablecloths. Give the dresser a polished look by touching it up with color paint and hardware embellishments.

Flat plastic containers: You can stack linens in these containers that you can easily stow under the bed, next to your seasonal sweaters and stored gift wrap. Make sure to roll your linens around cardboard tubes before securing with rubber bands to keep them from getting wrinkled.

Pantry: You can set aside a shelf in your pantry for holding an open rack or bin, or a laundry basket that holds your linens. You can also drape the linens on extra wide hangers, which you will hook onto a shower rod installed inside the pantry to reduce fold lines on larger tablecloths.

Fine-tune the way you organize and store your fine china

Follow these steps in making sure your dining room is safe from clutter due to fine china breakage:

Make sure everything is well-cushioned against chips and cracks with the help of protective padding. See to it that a felt sheet or a thin foam is sandwiched between stacked plates, bowls, and saucers, and remember to nestle your dishes inside china storage containers that come with soft sides for extra cushion.

Never pile more than eight dishes together. Keeping stacks small ensures they do not slide, smash, and create clutter. Having big piles of plates also places unnecessary stress on the plates at the bottom.

Keep your fine china stored in an area with the least amount of traffic. While storing them in a dining room cabinet or hutch is the easiest solution, you could also make use of your linen closet's unused shelf, an unused spot below the guest bed, or a temperature-controlled basement or attic. What is important is that you choose a spot that is not in the way of family activities and that will prevent your fine china from being jostled and jumbled.

Store cups right side up or hang them on hooks. Because the rims of fine china cups tend to easily get damaged, placing them in an upside-down position makes it more likely for them to get scratches and nicks.

Take extra caution in putting china on display on an open shelf. A hutch can look charming when filled with your fine china collection, but you have to make sure its shelves come with defined grooves that your dishes' edges can sink into. This will prevent them from rolling and slipping into a big, broken mess, as well as keep them from crowding and banging alongside each other.

Reclaim your dining room's welcoming feel
Reduce clutter in the dining room to make it more inviting to eat in by ditching the following items:

Bent flatware: You can always polish tarnished flatware pieces, but you have to let go of forks with tines that are embarrassingly twisted out of shape. Get rid of flatware that you no longer use, especially if the space in your utensil drawer is all maxed out.

Unusable tablecloth: They include the ones that are badly stained, hideously covered with wax drippings, or not the right size or shape for the dining table. Unless you can have them cleaned or repaired, you have to get rid of these items.

Special occasion china: While it is great to own beautiful china, especially ones that have a special meaning to you, they will only end up creating clutter if you do not really use them that frequently. Keep a single piece from a set to display in your dining room, then give all other pieces to a relative who will get to use them more frequently than you do.

Specialty glassware: Your elegant martini glasses should have no place in the dining room if they take up too much space and do not even get used at all. Commit yourself to keeping just one set of glassware that you know you will use often and give up the rest.

Single-use items: It might seem convenient to have disposable utensils, dishes, and servingware around in the dining room, but they are not friendly both to the environment and your hosting budget. Stick to salad tongs, carafes, casserole dishes, and other quality items that are easy on the pocket and do away with clutter-causing disposables.

Duplicate servingware: You will lose precious space in your dining room if you let the hoarding bug get the best of you. Do away with non-essential pieces, keep just one of everything, and give the duplicates to friends or relatives.

Old place cards: Keep clutter to a minimum by keeping just one set of place cards that you feel you should hold onto. Give the rest to someone who will have better use for them.

Harsh lighting: A little help from some mood lighting is all it really takes to enjoy most meals with your family. You do not need to go wild with crazy colors, as a dimmed light can easily transform a cafeteria-like meal into one that feels cozy. Let go of glaringly bright lights and use dimmable bulbs instead.

Struggling plant life: Indoor plants that look like they are about to die will not do your meals any good. Whisk them off to another part of the house that can provide them better light.

Kill All Clutter in Your Kitchen

Most likely, you and your family spend a lot of time in the kitchen, making it one of the most cluttered rooms in your house. Declutter your kitchen in no time with the help of these tricks:

Keep your kitchen counter organized

Corral counter clutter in your kitchen by:

Adopting a clean-in-a-flash strategy
If what you do in the kitchen involves more than simply preparing meals and eating, you need to establish a plan for when homework, keys and coins, laptops, and other non-kitchen-related items have to be cleared out as quickly as possible because dinnertime has come. You can use shallow baskets to swiftly gather worksheets, books, pencils, tablets, and other items; all you have to do next is to take the goods out of the kitchen.

Enlisting the help of your kitchen walls
The walls in your kitchen can aid you in making sure your counter remains clutter-free. You can have a hook rack mounted on a wall to hold pots, pans, dishtowels, and oven mitts. A wall-mounted knife rack would also be great to have in your kitchen, as this lets you do away with the knife block that tends to take up too much space on the counter.

Editing your collection of kitchen appliance
When you really think about it, you would realize that you do not actually need to have a popcorn maker, electric kettle, or rice cooker sitting on the kitchen counter. It's important to evaluate how often you use an appliance, and if you even use them at all. Once you have determined that, after letting your juicer sit and gather dust for over a year, you are not a juice drinker, then you can freely admit to yourself that it is high time you gave it up. And, when

you're done paring down your kitchen appliances, decide on which item deserves a spot on the counter, depending on whether you will be using it daily or nearly every day. This is the reason it would be a good idea to invest in an appliance garage cabinet, which can store your smaller appliances but still have them within easy reach. But, if you do not have a space to dedicate to storing kitchen appliances, consider getting a rolling cart in which you can store your hand mixer, microwave, and other devices.

Making use of turntables and trays

Small items like bud vases, olive oil cruets, and condiment jars can easily cause clutter when placed on your kitchen counter. Contain the visual mess by holding them all in a tray that has a shallow lip; pick one that will complement the décor on your kitchen. Put your spices on a turntable to help keep them in order as well as to spice up the look of your kitchen counter.

Preparing a paper pile catcher

The kitchen counter tends to collect lots of non-food items, including papers and mail. It would be wise to purchase a few stackable letter trays to hold and help you sort bills, magazines, and the kids' papers. A lidded box would be a better option if you usually collect coupons and receipts, as the lid will hide everything inside while keeping your kitchen counter looking organized and clutter-free.

Tidy up your collection of cookware, kitchen gadgets, and knives

Keep them from ruling over your kitchen by practicing these decluttering techniques:

Pots and pans – Stow these heavy, bulky items without a hitch.

Pot rack: A pot rack that you can mount on the kitchen ceiling is an effective storage solution for your pots and pans. You can easily find one that suits the size of your kitchen, so that the only issue you will have to deal with is hanging the pot rack where it will not hit a person in the head. A good spot to hang the contraption is beside a wall, above an island, or in a corner.

Pull-out cabinet: A pullout cabinet makes it easy for you to store your saucepans and skillets in a narrow space like beside the refrigerator. Make sure to install many hooks so that you can hang the lids separately.

Wall shelf: One that comes with hooks along its bottom will provide you dual benefits—you may stack your pans and pots (with lids on) on top, and you can leave extra kitchen tools or cookware hanging from the hooks below. Pick a wall shelf made of a material that could endure exposure to moisture, scratches and scuffs, and heavy duty use. Stainless steel, enamel, and coated wire are great choices.

Lazy Susan: This will be a big help in keeping your cookware within easy reach, especially when placed in a kitchen cabinet of the deep corner type. Just see to it that it is wide enough to accommodate long-handled pots, to avoid having the pots get in the way with the spinning action by banging against the walls.

Pegboard wall: You can mount a painted pegboard sheet on a blank wall, then attach S-hooks on it for hanging your pots.

Kitchen gadgets – Kitchen gadgets tend to get tossed inside the drawer, which usually means you end up frantically poking around for that apple corer or potato peeler.

Utensil crock: A utensil crock is an extremely useful gadget for storing ladles, spatulas, whisks, and other tools that come with handles. Make sure to keep your utensil crock beside the stove to make it easier for you to grab the tool you need, even if you do not move an inch away from the stove.

Wall receptacles: Create wall receptacles for your kitchen gadgets by having a small shelf mounted on a wall, then adding shallow trays or bins to hold the gadgets out of sight but within easy reach. You might also try using durable wall pockets, which you can purchase from office supplies stores, for the same purpose.

Drawer dividers: Round up your oddly shaped kitchen stuff, which include funnels, pot scrapers, and twine, by installing a drawer divider inside your kitchen drawer. You could go for the two-tier stacking drawer divider model to provide twice the storage space, if the depth of your drawer allows it.

Knives – When storing knives, it is all about safety and sharpness, which is why you need to choose a space where you can grab a knife without accidentally cutting yourself and where blades will not get nicked or dull. To achieve that, you will want the following:

Knife block: A knife block is a portable and convenient place to store your knives in. Choose one that lets you stick in the knives as you wish instead of the conventional type that comes with defined slots.

Magnetic wall rack: This is a great idea if you do not have small children in the house—a magnetic strip is mounted on the kitchen wall and serves to hold knives in that spot, saving you plenty of cabinet and drawer space.

Pullout drawer: This special drawer, which can be purchased or get custom-made, helps keep knives sorted because it comes fitted with slots in different sizes. To protect smaller kids in your home, make sure to secure the pullout knives drawer with a locking device that is designed to be child-proof.

Keep clutter from drowning inside your kitchen drawer

Heed these tips for making sure your catch-all drawer is not a perpetual tangled mess:

Keep only the essential junk

Try taking out items from your kitchen drawer and then transferring them to another drawer in the house, which could be in the bathroom or the bedroom. When you use your kitchen drawer for holding only those items that you tend to use regularly, you keep potential clutter from living there in the first place.

Consider customizing inside

Evaluate the things that need to be stored in your kitchen drawer, and think about customizing the drawer by using smaller containers inside the main organizer. This way, you can fit specific items, instantly creating a distinct space for each item, maximizing the entire space in the drawer, and making it easier for you to look for any item when you need to.

Think of location

Location is everything not just in real estate, but in the kitchen drawer as well. You will easily and quickly get to your most frequently used items if you place them front and center, and simply keep the rarely used ones in the back. You will significantly cut down on the time you spend looking for items if you just organize your kitchen drawer depending on how frequent you use them.

Take advantage of standard wire organizers

Because it is designed to be deep, a wire metal organizer makes for an effective kitchen drawer organizer. You can just snip open sections with the aid of a wire cutter to tailor it to your exact storage needs. If you do not prefer its stainless steel color, you can just go over the entire thing with color paint.

Zone in on your pantry

Organizing the pantry by sections lets you easily determine what foods you already have, what needs to be restocked, and where your next purchases should go. Figuring out the food categories in your pantry will greatly help reduce the time it takes for you to prepare a meal, as well as reduce the amount of clutter you might make in the process.

General food storage: See to it that you have enough room to store general food staples, which usually have a longer shelf life. Group food items according to type (soups, fruits, veggies) and organize them on the shelf in rows. Consider using stair-step shelves to help keep the cans in the back row in sight.

Quick breakfasts: Organize your morning staples in a spot that is easily accessible to help you find all the food items you need before you have even inhaled your cup of coffee. You can fit breads inside an under-shelf basket and utilize a double-decked turntable to make use of a corner space. Set aside the shelf space for boxed items like instant oatmeal, cereals, and pancake mixes.

Lunch on-the-go: Non-edible items should also have their room in your pantry, especially if they are what you need to use regularly to prepare lunch. Keep napkins, Ziploc bags, disposable utensils, and other lunch items stored in their own section to speed up the packing process. Organize them inside a handled basket so it is easy for you to grab them all at once, especially when you are pressed for time on most mornings. This also makes everything easier to manage when you have to prepare a quick lunch on a busy weekend.

Effortless weeknight meals: If you love meal planning, this idea will send you through the roof. Once you are done shopping for groceries, fill several sturdy bins with seven days' worth of dinner items, then place the bins front and center in the pantry. Make sure to divide every bin by meal to make it easier for you to start cooking every time. You can also use the same method when stocking the fixings you need to prepare chicken noodle soup, spaghetti and meatballs, and other family favorites.

Easy entertaining: Having a section for food items you will need for emergency entertaining will help you prepare a meal without being too stressed about it as well as avoid creating a big mess, making you feel more stressed with all the decluttering you will have to do afterwards. Stock different kinds of quick-fix appetizers, trays, napkins, and toothpicks in baskets, which you will store on the top shelf to get them out of the way of your everyday food items. When your unexpected guests drop by, simply pull down a basket and whip up a meal pronto.

Baking goods: Use see-through, airtight containers that can easily be stacked to store your dry baking ingredients, then place them in the baking goods section of the pantry. Organize other ingredients like frostings and mixes nearby by stacking them on top of one another with the help of pantry shelf risers.

Kitchen tools & appliances: Avoid taking up shelf space in your pantry for storing cookware. You can hang bulky utensils as well as those that you do not use every day from hooks installed at the back of the kitchen door or on a wall.

Tame your refrigerator

The refrigerator is one of the major sources of clutter in the kitchen, which includes forgotten leftovers, expired products, and old bottles. Follow these steps in decluttering and organizing your refrigerator once a month:

Clean and disinfect all surfaces

You need to make sure all surfaces inside your refrigerator is thoroughly cleaned and disinfected before you can go through the actual decluttering and organizing process. Doing so not only makes everything look nice and tidy, but it also lowers the risk of contamination and foodborne illnesses. Disinfect inside the fridge by:

Removing all contents

Getting everything out of the refrigerator ensures you will thoroughly wipe down each surface to get rid of stains, dirt, and congealed spills. If you worry about food spoiling, try working in sections or putting perishable foods in an ice-filled cooler while you are cleaning the fridge.

Wear them down with wipes

Use either a disinfecting spray with paper towels or disinfecting wipes to sanitize every surface inch inside your refrigerator. Make sure to include all shelf levels and inside all door compartments. Remove the drawers and soak in a tub filled with hot, soapy water; give them a good wipe-down before putting them back in.

After reassembling the refrigerator, add a deodorizer inside to clear away any lingering unpleasant odors. You can use baking soda or those special fridge packs that you simply place, opened, at the back or stick to the wall.

Declutter the fridge
Mentally evaluate your refrigerator's layout, then work your way section by section.

Door decluttering tips – The door is your refrigerator's warmest part, which is why condiments are the only items that should be placed there. Although many people tend to this, it is not a good idea to place milk and eggs (they belong somewhere colder) in the refrigerator door. What do belong here are your less-perishable food items, such as condiments, butter, and sauces. Keep them organized and clutter-free with these tips:

Store condiments in an egg carton
Line the bottom of the fridge door section you plan to use with an egg carton. Put in your bottled ketchup, mayonnaise, mustard, and dressing in an upside down position. Doing so ensures they are organized and clutter-free, as all of their liquid components are sitting near the bottle openings. Now you no longer have to coax your condiments out of their containers by shaking or tapping.

Divide the door into sections and label accordingly
Keeping items truly organized is easy when you make sure like items are placed together in the same divider, then labeled with a magnet or sticker. Try this method with your dressings (e.g. mustard, ketchup, relish, mayonnaise), sauces (e.g. soy sauce, hot sauce, barbecue sauce), or specialty items (e.g. tapenade, olives, pesto).

Place kids drinks in one of the door's bottom shelves
Give your kids easy access to their own "refueling zone" by filling a bottom shelf with their favorite drinks.

Upper shelf decluttering tips – The topmost section of your refrigerator is where the upper shelves are, so you would not want to keep any vegetables or raw meat there. What you can store up there are your deli meats, cheeses, drinks, yogurts, other ready-to-eat items, and leftovers, all of which have shorter shelf lives than butters, oils, or condiments.

Look for food easily through a Lazy Susan
At the back of the refrigerator are a multitude of long-forgotten food items, for the simple reason that it is hard to access them. Use your Lazy Susan to store and easily get to snacks, opened jars, and condiments as needed.

Hang baskets on the wall
Use suction cups to stick baskets to one wall of the refrigerator. You can fill them with string cheese, cheese rollups, hummus cups, lunch meat, and other small food items.

Create a box for foods nearing their expiry dates
Get a box, stick onto it a label that says "Eat Me Now", and fill with items that are about to expire.

Lower shelf decluttering tips – The lower shelf is where you can safely store your raw packaged meats and other raw ingredients, since they are just below your ready-to-eat items.

Make use of curtain ring clips
You may find wire bars or shelves on the edges of your refrigerator's shelves. Utilize the space below these shelves by hanging lettuce, shredded cheese, and other bagged items from their edges with the help of curtain ring clips.

Keep like items in same containers
Use clear baskets to ensure like items are grouped together and easily accessed. Fill the baskets with smoothie ingredients, sandwich fixings, sauces, or leftover food.

Store snacks in file organizers
You probably have file boxes lying around, so why not label and use them to keep all sorts of snacks like yogurt cups, pouch drinks, chopped veggies, and applesauce pouches.

Crisper drawer decluttering tips - The crisper drawer is usually temperature and humidity controlled to extend the shelf life of fresh foods in your refrigerator.

Use paper towels as liners
A crisper drawer tends to be the one of the nastiest areas to clean in the refrigerator, so keep it cleaner for longer by lining its bottom with sheets of paper towel prior to storing your vegetables and fruits. The paper towel will catch any bits of onion peel or lettuce that could fall off later on, so remember to swap for new sheets every week for easy cleaning.

Take advantage of drawer dividers
Dividers that you usually use in your clothing drawers will do their job in the crisper drawer as well. Go for the customizable ones that let you group spinach, lettuce, and other greens in one section, snap peas and carrots in another, and garlic, onions, and ginger in another.

Know the highs and lows of humidity
The correct use of your crisper drawers' humidity settings will help keep veggies and fruits fresher for longer, so set the humidity in one drawer to high and the other drawer to low. Then fill the high humidity crisper drawer with herbs, arugula, spinach, and other leafy greens, which will retain their crisp and freshness for a longer time from all that moisture. Avocados, apples,

pears, and other vegetables and fruits that give off ethylene gas should go to the low humidity crisper drawer to prevent them from ripening and rotting faster.

Prevent freezer clutter from ruining your life

It may seem like you never have enough space in your freezer, whether you own a drawer freezer, deep-freeze chest, or side-by-side freezer. Keep your freezer decluttered and more effective in storing foods by following these tips:

Put a label on everything

Labels help you keep track of what is inside the freezer, as well as when they were placed there or when they should be used.

Freeze individual portions

This will let you avoid having to thaw out a bag full of items when all you need is a small amount. Divide your ingredients beforehand and freeze individually, and simply take out what you need in cooking.

Keep things flat

An effective way of storing plenty of food in the freezer is to use quart- or gallon-sized freezer bags. Simply fill a bag with food, remove the air pockets, and lay flat in the freezer. Once the bags are frozen, stand them up on the sides to save more on space.

Make use of milk containers

Hold off on getting rid of empty milk cartons, as they are useful for storing regularly used veggies in the freezer. You can have those veggies laid out flat on cookie sheets and then frozen; afterwards, pour them into the milk cartons. This way, you can just easily grab exactly how much vegetables you need to cook.

Monitor freezer contents

Make sure to regularly check on what are inside the freezer by keeping a list or dividing the freezer into sections and simply monitoring them.

Use a vacuum food sealer

Avoid discovering yet another frostbitten bag holding unrecognizable food with the aid of the food sealer. Use it to secure freezer bags, making sure to remove all air pockets before sealing to help you identify the contents easily.

Defrost regularly

You need to defrost your freezer on a regular basis to avoid ice buildup.

Take advantage of magazine holders

After you have frozen flat your favorite sauces or meals, you can store them in magazine holders standing up or laid on the side. Make it easy for you to identify what is inside each holder by attaching a laminated label on the outside.

Organize with dry erase labeling
Dry erase markers make organizing the contents of your freezer a breeze, especially if your freezer is placed in a utility room or in the garage. Update your list every time you add something to the freezer or remove something from it.

Store items in plastic bins
Most stores sell clear plastic bins for less than a dollar, so buy several containers of the same size to help you keep together like items such as beef and poultry. Give all stored foods their individual spaces by labeling or decorating them.

Remove those boxes
A large number of frozen items are usually sold in big bulky boxes. Transfer the foods in a plastic crate or bin and get rid of the boxes.

Repurpose binder clips
You can store your freezer bags using binder clips if your freezer comes with slotted shelves. Doing so creates more space on the freezer's bottom shelf.

Line to keep clean
Use wrap that you simply press and seal to line your freezer shelves and to let you clean up any messes in a snap.

Store items in magnetized containers
Store smaller food items that you do not really use daily, like nuts and ginger, in magnetized containers placed in your freezer's top section.

Sort into bags
For a deep freezer, it would be great to sort the larger food items into shopping bags so that they are better organized and easier to pull out when needed.

Get rid of the shelves
Remove your freezer shelves if you find no use for them. This will open up more space inside your freezer and allow you to store more food in there.

Keep track of the shelf life
Having a full freezer can make it difficult to figure out which items should be eaten first. Solve this dilemma by keeping a list of foods and their corresponding shelf life in the freezer.

Store your spices smartly
While the right seasonings in the right amounts can quickly turn a dull meal into a delicious one, they are also prone to causing clutter in the kitchen. Organize your spices with the help of these tips:

Determine your space's best storage option

A 3-tier spice rack should be adequate for your daily cooking needs if you have a cabinet shelf to spare.

A mounted pull-down rack makes it easier to reach spices in the back row.
Magnetic wall strips work well in securing sealed spice cans onto wherever you need to use them.

Stock up and organize by cuisine
Buy your black pepper, salt, bay leaves, oregano, ginger, allspice, chili powder, chili powder, nutmeg, cumin, cinnamon, and other versatile spice staples in bulk. Then, organize in different variations of Indian spice trays (usually consisting of a circular metal tray with a lid, a tiny spoon, and seven small containers) for a clutter-free look and functional purpose.

Check your spices yearly
This will let you figure out which spice containers will have to be refilled and which need to be thrown out.

Do away with these kitchen mayhem-causing mistakes

Failing to put dishes away immediately
Your kitchen is likely to look more cluttered simply because there are dishes stacked in your dish rack or left in the sink. Do away with this issue by having family members agree running the dishwasher or looking for another place in which to sleep. This will let you simply unload the dishwasher the next morning while waiting for your brewed coffee to be made.

Using the refrigerator door as a gallery
Clutter will surely result from blanketing your refrigerator door with your children's colorful drawings, no matter how pleasing to the eye they might be. Try dedicating a gallery wall in the dining room, where you can hang your kids' framed artwork in rotation.

Not getting rid of containers
Odds and ends that no longer have value have to be tossed out of the kitchen, including chipped containers and cracked lids. Avoid collecting clutter in your kitchen by pulling unmatched pieces and worn and torn containers from all cabinets about twice a year. If you need to replace them, purchase clear containers that come with pourable, snap, and flip lids.

Placing electronics on the counter
Technology is a welcome addition in the kitchen, especially when it lets you watch your favorite cooking shows, get access to various cooking tips, and save your well-loved recipes. But what is not welcomed in your kitchen is technology being destroyed by the clutter in your counters, which include splatters, spills, and drips. Clear out your counters while protecting your smartphone, tablet, or laptop by setting them on mounted hangers or hooks; make sure to install them at eye level to allow for better viewing.

Not decluttering under the sink

That spot under your kitchen sink is easy to get cleared out with some help from smart storage pieces. Get everything out of the space first, then install a shelf, making sure it is elevated to maximize space. You can place your bottles of cleaning solution on an old lazy Susan or a caddy, and use additional trays as well as hooks to hold other cleaning necessities in plain view.

Banish Clutter from Your Bedrooms

Whether you like it or not, your bedroom is generally a dumping area for unpacked bags, dirty laundry, and various knickknacks. Because it is usually not a place that guests see, the bedroom inevitably gets the least bit of attention when it comes to decluttering around the house. Unfortunately, this exact place is where you should not allow clutter to accumulate, since it is where you go to get relaxed and sleep in peace. Keep clutter in the bedroom at bay with these tips:

Make use of storage-savvy organization solutions

Look for potential storage spots

It's easy to overlook a closet or any other thing you look at every single day in the bedroom, and it is just as easy to ignore the presence of damaged areas or the need for some good old decluttering. You might take photos from different angles of the bedroom closet, have the images printed, and figure out which spots are magnets for clutter, as well as which wall surface or corner is under-utilized. Doing so is an effective way of deciding on your ensemble for the next day and addressing your other wardrobe needs, such as organizing your jewelry, makeup, bags, shoes, and other regular-use bedroom items.

Use a multi-purpose nightstand

Because a bedroom usually falls short in terms of adequate square footage, it can be difficult to determine which furniture pieces should go in it. It is important that you choose pieces that are not only pleasing to look at, but also serve their purpose in the bedroom. This is why going for a multi-purpose nightstand is a great idea; a midsize one offers enough surface space to make sure your nighttime necessities are uncluttered, and enough drawers to keep your small clothing essentials organized.

Empty your dressers

A bedroom dresser usually receives enough care and attention in terms of decluttering, although it can still quickly turn into a messy maze of worn-out tees and mismatched socks. This is why you need to get every single item out of the closet once each season, and then go over every surface, nook, and cranny with your dust cloth and plenty of elbow grease. Make sure to segregate storage areas according to type or function, like putting all matched socks inside one drawer. You can place all your athletic socks in one narrow bin and your work socks in another. You might also try rolling your tees to help you look for a specific shirt quickly as well as keep your drawer looking mess-free.

Stow off-season items under your bed

If you do not live anywhere near a bench, then it would be reasonable to have your flip-flops go into hiding once cold weather season comes. On that note, you should also give your cozy sweaters and blankets a break once the heat is on during warm-weather months. Avoid having your off-season favorites take up valuable storage space in the bedroom by getting them out of the way and safely tucked under your bed. If you have a platform bed, you can take advantage of the storage capacity of decorative containers or matching baskets; otherwise, consider investing in underbed drawers that you can use to stash your coats, sweaters, and shoes and keep them decluttered.

Create a wardrobe wall

Most people may wish to have a bigger closet in their bedroom, but know that a traditional closet can be difficult to fit inside an existing bedroom. This is why it can be a good idea to create a wardrobe wall to address both your wardrobe and bedroom space needs. You might have the wall built out to have an opening included or have movable sections installed so you have lots of room for organization and storage. Save on square feet by using a curtain to cover your wardrobe wall instead of closing it with doors.

Clear out all surfaces in the bedroom

Decluttering your bedroom does not have to mean emptying out all your shelves and drawers. It can also mean turning your bedroom into a restful and serene space by visually decluttering all its open surfaces. Try putting only a lamp and a few pictures on display and keep clutter-causing pieces like jewelry, keys, and purses stored and organized.

Choose pretty storage containers

Most people use the kitchen organizing technique of taking items in odd-shaped containers and transferring them to other storage containers that can easily hold them. You can apply this same strategy in decluttering your bedroom's grooming spaces and dressers. Remove all unsightly containers and replace them with ones that do a fantastic job of decluttering, organizing, and decorative bedroom surfaces at the same time.

Make use of uniform baskets

You can easily swap and move around baskets of the same shape and size, depending on your standard closet configurations and personal needs. This idea is especially helpful when you are decluttering your bedroom, and you are strict about knowing the contents of your storage units as well as giving up items that you no longer use or have outgrown your needs. Uniform baskets also help cut down on visual clutter in your bedroom and contribute to an overall calming vibe.

Go sleek

Your bedroom tends to be a catchall area for bags, purses, and other odd-shaped stuff that are difficult to fit tidily onto shelves, resulting in a big bedroom mess. Give yourself a better way to evaluate and organize your possessions by taking advantage of narrow shelves, rows of hooks installed on a wall, and other slim spaces.

Maintain a cleared closet floor

While it is easy to just toss things on your closet floor, this practice can easily result in bedroom clutter. You can declutter your closet in no time by simply making sure the floor is always clear and clean.

Make use of drawer dividers

A lot of items in the bedroom, including pens, notebooks, moisturizers, and makeup brushes, need to be somewhere near your bed. The problem is that they end up causing major bedroom clutter. Ward off potential mess by using small dividers or containers on your nightstand, making sure they are cleared out three to four times a year. Throw out any item in multiples, such as bottles of body lotion, and anything past its best-by date, like makeup.

Keep your bedroom workspace clutter-free

Having a work space in the bedroom usually leads to losing your space for relaxation and sleep to lots of clutter. Fortunately, you can declutter your bedroom work space by:

Using attractive containers for keeping pens, pencils, and other frequently used items corralled
Stashing files in a closed patterned container
Keeping unaddressed paperwork in a bin

Part with your clothes

Clothes are one of the major sources of bedroom clutter, especially since people usually form an emotional attachment to particular garments. Make it easier for you to part with your clothes and declutter your bedroom by donating articles of clothing that have not seen the light of day for an entire year, having anything in need of repair taken to the tailor, and getting rid of anything that is worn out of shape.

Make use of your ceiling space

The fact that this storage space in your bedroom is not utilized that often doesn't have to mean you should forget about using it. For instance, that one square feet of space near the closet ceiling provides the right number of inches to accommodate baskets filled with out-of-season clothing or items your children have outgrown. Make sure to label everything so it is easier to determine what are contained in those baskets.

Use the correct hamper

It is essential that you have a hamper parked in the bedroom. Clutter in your place for rest and relaxation is mostly generated by dirty clothes that failed to make it to the laundry basket in the bathroom. But, you do not have to resign yourself to a conventional hamper, as you can always pick a sleek bin, a pretty basket, or something else that matches your bedroom décor.

Part with your jewelry

That saying about tossing any garment you have not worn in the last twelve months holds true for jewelry items, especially for those pieces that are broken beyond fixing. It would be better if you either get rid of it or donate it to someone who may find some other use for it. Whatever remains in your jewelry collection should be organized to keep them from getting tangled or lost. Try using a standup necklace storage solution and a multi-pronged bracelet holder, both of which are effective for decluttering and organizing jewelry.

Be open to creative bedroom storage strategies

The following storage ideas can help you maintain the peaceful, clutter-free atmosphere you seek in a bedroom:

Go for ladder-style shelving

Use a ladder-style shelf to hold different items in your bedroom. This type of storage unit offers open shelves of varying depths so you can organize everything from extra linens and blankets to décor and trinkets. The ladder-style's height also provides extra space for holding larger items.

Make use of easy open shelving

Remove your bedside table's bottom drawer to create an open shelf space that you can use to display small decorations and keepsakes, as well as to store various items that you can just grab and go.

Create a cozy grooming station

Create a primping corner in your bedroom by bringing in a vanity table that comes with storage drawers, a lamp, and a mirror to provide the right lighting for easy makeup application, decorative trays to hold items on top of the vanity, and a wall-mount organizing cabinet. Finish the whole space by adding a small stool you can easily tuck under the table to save on floor space and avoid visual clutter.

Put your accessories on display

There are certain accessories that look so cute it would be a shame to put them away in jewelry boxes. You can store as well as display your jewelry pieces instead on hooks installed on a bedside table or a dresser's side. Instead of getting the hooks installed the traditional way, try turning them to one side, as this lets you create more space for holding necklaces or bracelets as well as helps prevent them from getting all jumbled up.

Show off using a storage tower

Using a customizable storage tower allows you to organize various items as well as show off your treasured stuff. The storage tower's bottom half features a cabinet where you can store things, and its upper portion has shelves that are kept enclosed by a display case that comes with a protective glass door.

Take advantage of sitting storage

Your bedroom could use a bench that is sleekly constructed and comes with large drawers to store your seasonal clothing and extra blankets. Adding a plush helps create a comfy perch on which you could sit while putting on your socks and shoes every morning.

Get quirky with jewelry

You can use a corkboard that's covered with fabric to serve as a jewelry storage solution for your necklaces, and a metal grate to hold your earrings. Choose your preferred printed fabric and use to cover an entire corkboard. Keep those fancy necklaces intact with the help of cute pushpins. Meanwhile, create a vintage-looking holder for your earrings by framing an old vent cover or a metal grate.

Keep items hidden in plain sight

Bring a trunk into your bedroom's sitting area and use it to hold extra blankets and linens. Pick one that is covered with durable fabric so it feels comfortable when you are sitting on it, or putting your feet as you sip on your coffee or read a book.

Look under the bed for storage support

Keep bedroom items under the radar by storing them under the bed. You can use rolling bins to hide a multitude of things, including shoes, accessories, and out-of-season garments. To make sure each item stays in its designated home, label each container on its sides or top with removable stickers. You can also adapt old crates or dresser drawers for underbed storage purposes, as long as you make them effortless to grab and slide by attaching pulls and casters.

Get a boost from an extra dresser

Old dressers will look great in your bedroom if you paint them in the same color to match one another as well as the bedroom décor. You can further turn up their style factor by replacing all knobs with drawer pulls that match.

Make use of your credenza

A credenza usually finds itself belonging to a dining room, but that does not mean it cannot have its place in your bedroom. Add a jewelry box or pretty accessories on top of the credenza, then transform it into a charming dressing table by adding a lamp and hanging a mirror above it. Store your purses, books, and other items inside your beautiful storage unit.

Say yes to armoires

An armoire is considered a tried and tested storage unit for the simple reason that it adds style and elegance to any bedroom, aside from being able to hold everything from your TV and linens to clothes and accessories.

Bring in a bedside desk

Desks do not have to be confined to the office. You can add one to your bedroom space to use as a makeup vanity or as a nightstand. Fill its drawers with your bedside necessities and add a reading lamp on its tabletop.

Mount a bedside shelf on a wall

The bedside table is a great spot to start when decluttering your bedroom. Turn yours from being a mess consisting of empty water glasses, medicine bottles, chocolate wrappers, books, and magazines by storing only your bare necessities, which could be a bottle of water and an alarm clock. It also helps to remove that nightstand you have sitting on the bedroom floor; have a shelving unit mounted on a wall or get your headboard customized to house your bedside necessities instead. Consider installing magnetic boards over the makeshift nightstand to provide a space for displaying your cherished photos.

Do not ignore small spaces

If no space is available in your bedroom for a nightstand, you could carve out a recessed niche in a wall. After you drywall the spot, install shelves to hold books and accessories.

Create a bedside library

Turn a bedside table that comes with multiple drawers into a mini-library. Set aside the top drawer for storing only your cough drops, hand lotion, and TV remote.

Hook jewelry up on a wall

If you find that your jewelry box is running out of storage space, you can organize your precious accessories on hooks attached to a wall or on one side of your dresser. Five to six rows of hooks should be enough to showcase your favorites on rotation.

Ladder them all up

Have style and function meet by using a reclaimed ladder as a display space and storage solution for your collection of books, keepsakes, and potted plants. The advantage to this unconventional decluttering idea is that you could easily switch up what you want to display and store in it.

Make use of cubbyholes

Cubbyholes are great storage solutions because they can easily be adapted to your growing child's needs. A bench can currently function as a place for your kid to tuck his toys and books into, but later on he can outfit it with bins and baskets to keep his stored items concealed. You can create a storage bench for your child by turning an open-back style bookcase on its side, then attaching feet to the bottom and finishing all over with a fresh coat of paint.

Sort and hang

The simplest organization system you can use to declutter your child's clothes is simply sorting them for each day and draping them on labeled hangers suspended from hooks at the back of a closet door.

Play your clothes organizing cards right

Follow the tips below to always have something to wear while keeping clutter away.

Give clothes room to breathe

Stacking your clothes tidily or letting them hang freely helps retain their good looks. This is why it is essential that you donate unworn apparel to make room for a breathing space in your closets and drawers. Have smart closet systems, drawer organizers, and over-the-door racks installed to rein in your existing clothes and ward off clutter.

Store clothes in full view

Instead of armoire drawers or dressers, try using open shelves and bookcases to store your clothes. They allow you to have a quick view and offer an easy way to retrieve the garment you need. You can bring a bookcase into your closet to contain stacks of jeans, sweaters, and other foldable items. Try adding colorful baskets that are labeled to serve as shelving units for your delicates and socks.

Establish a closet rod system

This space will help you figure out which item goes where and allows you to search for what you need and return it to where it belongs quickly and easily. The closet rod system also lets you store together similar items to avoid stuffing too many garments in one spot; as a result, other garments avoid becoming wrinkled or falling off their hangers. Segregate your clothes into different sections with the help of handwritten tags that are held by colorful drapery rod and closet clips.

Keep clothes-mending tools on hand

Use matching storage solutions that look stylish and clutter-free to create a personalized closet system where all your apparel and clothes-maintenance tools are kept. You will have an easier time replacing any lost buttons, pressing a blouse, or stitching an unraveled hem if your mending kit, iron and board, and button jar are close by. Having the ability to repair and care for your clothes so easily helps you avoid having rumpled or damaged items taking up unnecessary space in the closet.

Adopt a pre-sorting system

Use wood hangers to organize your best garments and help them retain their shapes prior to bringing together your outfits for the next seven days, separating them conveniently with dividers that are labeled with the days of the week. This pre-sorting method allows you to give your garments a pre-check, adds time for fixing flaws or cleaning up spots before the first day of the week arrives, and makes it easier to get dressed even when you are pressed for time.

Make use of a door

Take advantage of multi-hook racks, over-the-door hooks, and shoe bags to hold your freshly pressed ensembles, regularly used coats, and baseball caps for the moment. You might also consider adding a pegboard to the back of the door, then add hooks in which you can organize your belts, neckties, and scarves.

Think outside the box

Optimize your family's clothes storage by taking advantage of hanging compartmentalized bags, storage bins and baskets, drawer and shelf organizers, specialty hangers and racks, and customizable closet systems. Create a personalized storage system for each family member by utilizing suitcases, wire planters, and vintage hat boxes to organize out-of-season garments, used clothing, and fashion accessories.

Make use of freestanding storage solutions
Add extra clothing storage options in the bedroom by bringing in roomy wardrobes and antique armoires, which you can easily customize with the addition of closet rods and modern storage bins.

Have fun customizing your kids' closet
Because little kids wear smaller garments, you can easily fit in more clothes inside their closets. Go for a multitier system that comes with dual rods. You can use the lower rod for holding your kids' play clothes and church clothes, and sort them using closet dividers. Finish by having an image sketched, stenciled, or painted on each drawer's interior to help your kids determine what is kept where.

Get creative with decluttering under the bed
Use fabric bags, wooden drawers, plastic boxes, and wire racks in storing extra robes, folded sweaters, balled up socks, special occasion shoes, or extra jeans under the bed.

Keep the following items away from your bedroom closet
You will thank your lucky decluttering stars that you followed these tips:

Extra hangers: Because hangers are inherently clunky, taking up too much space in your closet, you will be better off keeping only the number you need. Set aside one hanger each for each item of clothing you need to hang up, and eliminate the rest. When purchasing a new piece of clothing, commit to giving up one item you already own before draping the new one on the now-empty hanger.

Out-of-season clothing: While your favorite pair of fuzzy boots serves their purpose during winter, their bulkiness takes up valuable storage space in the warmer months. Keep your out-of-season articles stored under the bed or in the basement, and switch out items as needed.

Anything not your style: Your style may consist of pairing a black top with black jeans, or consistently wearing something with lace or embroidery on it, or simply putting on dresses all the time. The important thing is to make sure that everything you have in your closet has to reflect your style, so ditch all items that do not match your way of dressing. This idea actually helps you get dressed faster every morning, so it is a win-win.

Bulky coats: The reason the coat closet exists is because it was made to hold your bulky coats, parkas, outdoor blankets, and umbrellas. Get these items out of your bedroom closet to free up space as well as avoid letting water, dirt, and salt invade your place for sleep and relaxation.

Anything not worn for an entire year: You most probably have garments you have never worn even once, whether a deeply discounted item you got at the mall or a gift from your spouse. What is important here is that you should do away with any clothing that you have not worn in twelve months. The same goes for items that no longer fit you, are stained, or are threadbare.

Luggage: Keeping a suitcase nearby is a great idea, especially if taking spontaneous vacations is your thing. But instead of crowding your bedroom closet with luggage, try stashing it under the bed or up in the attic. Make use of the empty space in the suitcase by storing your extra linens or out-of-season clothing in there.

Outdoor accessories: Fill an attractive basket with your collections of scarves, mittens, and hats. Instead of hiding them in the closet drawer, showcase your basket of accessories by placing it by the bedroom door. Forgetting to bundle up yet again will now be a thing of the past.

Jewelry pieces: When displayed properly, you can turn your beautiful jewelry into art. Store your rings inside an elegant dish and your necklaces and chokers on a tree, but refrain from hiding them in the closet. It is usually crowded inside a closet, so it is easy to knock your jewelry pieces over while grabbing a shirt or pulling out a dress. Display your jewelry on the vanity instead.

Wedding dress: Whatever your reason may be for keeping your wedding dress after all these years, you need to store it somewhere besides your closet. Wedding dresses need to be kept under special storage conditions, and they can really take up a lot of space. Your best bet is to wrap it in a clean garment bag before storing under the bed or in the hall closet.

Animals and their toys: Your beloved pets, as well as their beds and toys, do not belong in the closet. Keep them out to protect your black trousers and suede boots from hair and claws.
Food gifts: Prevent mice and moths from showing up uninvited in your closet by not storing food gifts in it. It is best to keep all food items where they belong, which is in your kitchen.

Combat kid clutter creatively

Handle your children's clutter with grace by using these kid-friendly storage options:

Fun bins: Brightly colored bins are great for storing your kids' belongings and for making sure their bedrooms stay clutter-free. Arrange the bins so that your kids can easily reach for them. You can fit several bins snugly into a single oversized organizer, and then label each bin for easy identification of its contents.

Wall cubbies: Another effective solution for your child's decluttering needs is the use of display cubes. You can paint them in your child's favorite color and arrange them in his preferred configuration for a personalized look. A small wall or any vertical space would be a great location for a stack of cubbies filled with trinkets and collectibles.

Bookcases: Turn your child's bookcases into a central storage unit by placing them side by side. Fill the open shelves with toys and hide unsightly items in the built-in drawers. Make this storage solution work with any age and with any décor by painting it a creamy white.

Corner cabinet: Take advantage of unoccupied corners in the bedroom by using them to store clothes and other bedroom necessities. If you have a baby, you can bring a dresser into his nursery and turn it into a changing table. Fill the deep drawers with your baby's changing supplies and clothes.

Rolling bins: You can turn a simple rolling plastic bin into a storage solution for toys and other items that your child can use. It will fit perfectly under his bed and help make decluttering and cleaning your child's bedroom less difficult. Choose rolling bins that have casters and are made with a lightweight yet durable material to withstand all that pulling during playtime.

Metal locker: Your kids' bedroom can stay clutter-free and look visually appealing at the same time with a little help from flea market treasure finds. For instance, you can make use of a metal locker unit in holding your kids' extra clothes and toys in both closed and open storage, in keeping with your home's industrial aesthetic.

Food storage containers: Use a large bin to organize clear food storage containers containing small toys. Make it easy for your kids to know in which containers are specific items placed by sticking labels on top.

Cleaning caddy: Organize your children's art supplies while making them easily accessible by putting them inside a cleaning caddy. Pick one that comes with a handle to help you transport the art supplies from one room to another. You can segregate different types of color applicators by keeping like items in a plastic cup.

Keep your nightstand in a clutter-free state
Heed these tips on how to organize your nightstand:

Decide whether to toss out or keep an item: The nightstand is the last object you come in contact with before going to bed and is also what you initially see when you get up every morning. This is why it easily attracts all sorts of odds and ends. Edit your nightstand's contents on a daily basis to keep clutter away.

Organize your for-keeps items: Make sure to rid your nightstand of all items that you have no need of upon waking up or before going to sleep. Either transfer these items to a shelf or drawer, or place them somewhere else other than the bedroom.

Add efficiency to your nightstand: Organize the items you do need to have on hand before sleeping and upon waking up on your nightstand. If you usually read before turning in for the night, keep just one book on the nightstand and place other reading materials in a bookshelf. If you need to have a box of tissues, make sure to remove and dispose of the ones you've used.

Consider getting rid of your alarm clock: You probably could get away with not placing an alarm clock on your nightstand if you use the alarm feature on your smartphone.

Manage the cables around your nightstand: Make sure to secure the plugs and cords of your essential oil diffuser or white noise machine to one of the nightstand's legs to avoid making a tangled mess on the tabletop.

Use the right storage containers: You can keep your earrings, rings, watch, and eyeglasses in a small decorative dish or tray. If your nightstand comes with multiple drawers, you might want to place the less frequently used items in the lower drawers and the most often used in the topmost drawer.

Prevent potential drawer clutter by using drawer dividers: They help you find everything you need quickly, as well as make it easy for you to keep your nightstand looking tidy.

Beat the Clutter Out of Your Bathroom

With all the hair- and skin-cleaning products you use in the bathroom, it is no wonder that it's common for clutter to accumulate in there. Thankfully, there are ways to keep your bathroom looking clean and tidy.

Use practical bathroom storage solutions

Under the sink: Although drawers and doors cost more than open storage options, they do a great job in taming clutter in the bathroom. Consider using small drawers in dividing bath essentials by type or function.

Space above the toilet: That space above your toilet makes for a valuable spot for extra storage (think extra toilet paper rolls or bath towels).

Back of door: The back of your bathroom door is a potential space for storage and organization. You could install short cabinets behind the door and outfit them with magnets or slim caddies, or mount a pegboard with narrow hooks attached to it. You could then use either of the two options when storing your makeup tools and grooming supplies.

Makeup bins: You may find it hard to part with that favorite eye makeup you bought from way back, but it has probably expired by now and you can always buy a new one with better formulation or shade. Evaluate the contents of your makeup drawer twice a year, taking note of their expiration dates and whether or not they have become discolored or smell bad. After disposing of the expired products, organize the rest in clear makeup bins before returning to the drawer.

Pullout shelves: You will find it easier to keep your belongings organized if finding what you need is effortless. Consider having pullout shelves in your bathroom. You can store your toiletries in the shelves after outfitting them with clear baskets, which should be labeled for easier identification of contents.

Basket for cords: You probably have several corded items sitting in your bathroom that take up considerable space, including your curling irons and hair dryer. Because their cords usually get tangled so easily, they are notorious for causing clutter on the bathroom countertop on a daily basis. Try tucking the corded appliances into a basket, which you will stow out of sight after each use.

Towel hooks: Towel hooks are great for reducing visual clutter in the bathroom. Use them instead of bars in hanging your bath towels. People usually do not have the patience to hang their wet towels tidily on a bar anyway, and a towel hanging from a hook makes for a less distracting look.

Portable caddies: Your bathroom most likely houses grooming supplies that have all kinds of odds and ends mixed with them, making it harder to keep everything organized. You can use multiple portable caddies to contain your miscellaneous items and prevent clutter from taking over the bathroom.

Avoid messing up the bathroom countertop

Follow these strategies for maintaining a clear surface in your bathroom:

Arrange your toiletries on a beautiful tray. What is great about trays is that they help you create boundaries, so that your jars and bottles of bathroom products do not find their way to the countertop. You can buy pretty trays that are designed to hold bathroom items; otherwise, any tray will do, as long as it is resistant to moisture, completes the bathroom décor, and easy to clean.

Place cotton balls, cotton swabs, and other loose items in attractive canisters to keep them sanitary, clean, and neat. You can use mason jars, apothecary jars, or vintage tea tins to display those loose items. If you would rather not display them, consider storing loose items in stacking canisters, which you will stash inside a vanity cabinet.

Use drawer trays in organizing miscellaneous items like bobby pins, headbands, and toe spacers, which usually find their way on countertops and stay there gathering dust and creating clutter. Choose drawer trays that come with dividers to make it easier to sort everything.

Mount toothbrush holders and soap dispensers on a wall instead of having them sit on the bathroom countertop, where they are likely to take up lots of room and create clutter. Get things even more streamlined by going for an all-in-one holder that can accommodate different items all at once, including soap bottles, toothbrushes, and tumblers.

Have a wall shelf installed in the bathroom, making sure it is slim to further reduce visual clutter. You can add a basket for toiletries if you would not want these items to be displayed. If you are lucky enough to have extra wall space, especially if it is close to the bathtub, consider anchoring to the space a full bookshelf that will be used to store your bathroom essentials as well as to serve as a display area for some of your favorite decorative items.

Optimize the space inside your medicine cabinet

Unlock the medicine cabinet's storage potential with these tricks:

Keep like items together to help you avoid having to frantically search for the dental floss, toothpaste, and mouthwash every morning. Make everything look even more clutter-free and visually appealing by using the same container in multiples, whether they are clear plastic tumblers or white ceramic cups. Your medicine cabinet will look even more polished if you paper the back with a stick-on shelf liner.

Use risers to let you keep twice as many items in the same space. Choose ones that are made with acrylic to give the appearance of not taking up too much space in the medicine cabinet.

Make use of mini jars to contain smaller items like ear swabs, nail clippers, mini hair elastics, and barrettes.

Take advantage of the medicine cabinet's underside by installing stick-on hooks to hang various items like bracelets, necklaces, or headbands.

Get creative with storing your toiletries

Small spaces and high humidity contribute to chaos in the bathroom. Here's how you can declutter this part of your home effectively:

Bring a touch of personality and plenty of storage to any awkward space by installing floating shelves. You can use a pair to store extra linens as well as put décor items like bath oil bottles and pretty perfume bottles on display.

Set aside a specific storage container for your styling tools by hanging a bin over your bathroom door. This way, your flat irons and hot blow dryer are off the counter as well as easily accessible. Make sure the bin you use is a heat-resistant one.

If your sink is surrounded by countertop space, you could add a platter to hold your often-used toiletries. Pretty vases and cups will do a great job holding combs and brushes and keeping them off the countertop.

Make use of the space available under the bathroom sink by sliding in metal bins or wicker baskets (lined with canvas) that can hold toiletries or hand towels. You can also turn one side of a vanity into prime real estate for towels by installing hooks or a towel bar.

Get the Clutter Out of Your Garage

One of life's most difficult situations has to be figuring out how to declutter your garage, since it is where the stuff you do not want inside the house usually end up. Make your mission to clear out garage clutter as painless as possible by following the guide below.

Gauge how the weather is
Decluttering your garage means you will need to haul everything outside and pile them on your driveway, which is why it would be best to do it when the weather is nice and dry. But because the unexpected always happens, such as rain, you will need to prepare tarps to quickly cover your belongings in case a sunny day turns sour. It also helps to have all family members pitch in when you do declutter the garage, especially since many items in this space tend to be bulky and, therefore, harder to handle on your own.

Prepare yourself for the hard questions
As you go through each item in your garage, ask yourself whether or not you actually need it, and if you do, would you keep it for a short amount of time or for the long term. You should also ask yourself if you can afford to replace a particular item, and if this is the case, then you can freely decide to let go of that item.

Divide the garage into sections
This space is where you place all sorts of items belonging to different categories, so you need to create separate areas for every storage type. You might want to categorize your belongings into these themes:

Car equipment
Lawn and garden
Sporting goods
Workbench tools

When you are done getting all items in the right order, segregate them further into the Keep, Donate, or Toss sections. Make sure to throw out duplicates of any item, to inspect the expiration dates for all gardening and lawn care chemicals, and to integrate the same hings in a single package so they end up taking less space in the garage.

Pick the right storage options
Choose storage that lets you work with the natural structure of your garage, especially if it has rafters or a high ceiling that make a garage the ideal space for overhead and vertical storage solutions.

Have plenty of bags to go around. They will enable you to commit to recycling on a regular basis, which is helpful in taming clutter and staying organized. Install a metal hook at the back of the garage door and hang your reusable bags there. You can also mount a dispenser on a wall near the door and fill it with plastic bags. It would likewise be a great idea to put up a wire basket from which you can grab paper bags.

Stock smaller garage items such as brushes, tape, sponges, and rags in clear plastic bins. They are easy to keep organized and do not cost much to acquire.

You will find a utility cart extremely useful, not just in handling a wide array of accessories, but also in moving things around since it is easy to maneuver. To make it easier and faster for you to clean up the car in your garage, make sure to outfit the utility cart with squeegees, chamois, and cleaners.

Get a shower caddy in a handheld style to help you corral your cleaning supplies in a portable and durable manner. Keep things organized by picking a caddy that comes with divided compartments.

Set aside a specific spot in which you will keep a collection of items you would prefer to recycle but are unable to put in the curbside bin. These can include CFL bulbs, batteries, and oil-based paints. You can utilize small bins in keeping like items together as well as shelves in storing chemicals. Keep recyclable items organized in a cabinet that is mounted on a wall, which will help in keeping your children and pets from getting access to them.

Make cleaning up in the garage an easy task by mounting a towel dispenser on a wall and keeping one to two bottles of cleaners on hand. You can buy an inexpensive dual purpose cleaning caddy that has an organizer for supplies as well as a holder for paper towels.

Avoid having to look for missing attachments once again by attaching to one side of your workbench a heavy duty magnetic tool holder.

Hide unsightly garage storage items by placing them in a corner and then covering with curtain panels that are attached to a rod.

Get things clearly organized in the garage by taking inspiration from the kitchen and making use of your extra spice containers. You can place washers, nails, and screws in those petite canisters that you always thought were too precious to throw out. The clear lids on these objects will help you have an easier time knowing what they contain, so you automatically save precious time when searching for something you need to use right away. Consider mounting a magnetic panel onto a pegboard and stick the canisters onto it after each use.

Having a metal locker in your garage allows you to have a safe place to store your instruction manuals, warranty information, and car maintenance guides. Make sure all these documents stay organized by placing them in storage files and magazine holder that have been labeled. You can also display reminders, articles, or sketches inside the locker by using message clips.

Attach a pegboard panel across a wall in your garage. Mounting it right above your workbench or a shelving unit offers a convenient way for you to hang and display your hammers, screwdrivers, and other tools. Make sure to use metal hooks instead of plastic ones, which will easily give in to wear and tear.

Hold a garage sale

A garage sale is not about selling your junk to unsuspecting neighbors who may happen to pass by your driveway. The first thing you have to do is to sort all garage items carefully, then to make it known that you are putting them up for sale. Evaluate each item as you go, being careful to set aside those items that are sellable like home goods, furniture, baby gear, and sports equipment. Try advertising on Garagesalestracker.com to help your garage sale gain more foot traffic. It also helps if you hold the sale around when people get their paychecks and are more willing to spend.

Let others use up the rest

One organization that would love to receive your donations is Habitat for Humanity, which will accept paints and tools. There are also community green spaces and garden clubs that welcome donations of old pots, leftover soil, and yard equipment.

Avoid bringing these items into the garage

Alcohol: You may be tempted to bring your twenty-four packs of beer into the garage because it takes up too much space in the kitchen, but beer, just like wine, easily freezes in cold conditions. On the other hand, exposure to light can cause beer to turn foul, while heat will turn wine into vinegar. It would be best to store your alcoholic beverages in a dark and cool place.

Canned food: The garage is actually a convenient place to store your extra non-perishable items, such as cereals and canned tuna, particularly when you are buying them in bulk. The problem is that the temperature in the garage constantly rises and falls, causing bacterial growth in your canned goods. Critters are also known to get into cardboard packaging like cereal boxes without trouble. Your best bet would be to store these items in the pantry.

Paint cans: Leaving paint in extreme temperatures can make it unusable, while exposure to moisture can cause the can that contains it to rust. This is why it would be better if you stored any leftover paint in the basement instead, unless your garage is equipped with a climate control mechanism.

Plywood: You may be able to store plywood in the garage, provided that you will be using it at the soonest possible time for a project. But, ditch this idea if you are planning to keep the plywood pieces sitting in the garage for a long while. Being exposed to moisture and temperature fluctuations can easily warp wood, especially when it does not have proper support while in storage.

Propane: While you hate the idea of running out of gas right in the midst of your barbecue, it just isn't worth risking your family's safety as a result of keeping your propane tank inside the garage. Look for a spot with good ventilation away from the house, seeing to it that the tank is in good condition. You can then just leave the tank outside, covered and sitting next to the grill, during the winter months.

Bring Order Back Into the Attic and Basement

Besides the garage, the attic and basement will have to be most cluttered areas in your home. Your family probably uses them both as a giant closet that holds all kinds of occasional-use items as well as pure junk. To bring order back to your attic and basement, read and follow these tips:

Have the following items on hand: All-purpose cleaner/other cleaning agents, duster, label tape, permanent marker, paper shredder, large boxes, trash bags, rags, paper towels, plastic storage boxes, shelving units, broom, and vacuum cleaner.

Clean up everything first
The attic quickly and easily collects dust, so go over the entire area with a synthetic duster to remove all traces of dirt. Make sure to reach all wooden beams, windows, frames, baseboards, columns, and walls. Clean the duster immediately once it becomes too dirty. Remember to dust your attic space's fans and other fixtures, which will be easier to get to if you use a duster that has an extension arm attached to it.

Use a vacuum to go over all surfaces and corners of your attic and basement. This is an effective way of removing dust mites, allergens, dander, and dead insects.

Use a cleaning solution to effectively scrub dirty basement floors. Try mixing detergent and ammonia with warm water, then apply the solution to the floor surface using a brush with stiff nylon bristles. Avoid using a metallic brush, as its metallic fibers can become trapped in the concrete, causing your basement floor to rust. Rinse everything with a hose before air-drying and vacuuming any excess moisture.

Break up the decluttering activity into mini-tasks
This is really effective, especially if you find it difficult to spend the entire day decluttering without feeling overwhelmed. For example, you can clear and wipe down the surfaces on the first day, box up the collected items the next day, and sweep the floors and wash the windows on the third day. Keep in mind that spending a whole week finishing the process will give you the same outcome.

Gather all the items you plan on selling
Transfer them into another part of the house, such as the garage, with the purpose of cleaning and sorting them so that they are likely to be bought at the best prices. Donate all items that did not entice any buyer instead of bringing them back into your home.

Sort effectively using a couple of large boxes
Set one of the large boxes for trash, another for items that you will donate, and the last one for your "probably" items. Fill each of these boxes as you move around the attic and the basement. Once the "probably" box is full, store for six months, then donate if you never used anything in it within that period.

Buy plastic totes, waterproof storage boxes, and shelving units
This is to store and organize everything in an orderly manner, as well as to get things off the attic or basement floor. You can buy shelving at different price points in various materials, including wood, plastic, and metal. You can also purchase stackable plastic totes with 18-gallon capacity in different colors at home improvement stores.

Open all storage containers sitting in the attic and basement.
Take out their contents and sort according to whether you will keep, donate, or throw them away. Place all items that need to be stored in a waterproof box, then add a label on top of the box to note its contents. Stack all filled and sealed waterproof boxes on your shelving. Make sure to recycle the paper, plastic bags, and cardboard boxes that are left behind.

Remember to clean out all closets and cupboards
Sort their removed items into the three large boxes, then wipe down, sweep, and vacuum inside the cleared closets and cupboards before returning all their contents.

Shred sensitive documents for peace of mind
Use the paper shredder to destroy your old documents that carry sensitive information, including your old bills, tax return files, credit card statements, and other documents that carry your personal info (e.g. Social Security number and banking details). Dispose of the shredded paper in disposable plastic bags.

Decide and sort as you go
Make up your mind about where everything should go while you are in the process of decluttering. If an item does not belong to any of the three large boxes, in the attic, or in the basement, it likely has to be stored in another part of the home, like your garage or a linen closet, so that you can quickly find it when you need it.

Leave Clutter Out of Your Laundry Room

You may have a laundry room that features lots of storage space or it may just be a corner down in your basement, but it is essential that you keep this space decluttered and clean. Doing the laundry in the middle of clutter will have you working longer and feeling stressed. Make your laundry room a mess-free space by following these tips:

Bring out the trash
Look around the workspace, washer, and dryer to determine what you should dispose of. You

will be amazed by the number of items that never made it to the garbage can. Ditch all of the damaged laundry hampers, broken hangers, dryer lint, empty detergent containers, expired laundry products, and pocket trash you could find. Make sure to have a trash can parked inside the laundry room to catch all potential clutter-causing items.

Clear out the space

You are probably wondering why the dryer in the laundry room is surrounded by basketballs, library books, and garden tools, but this is usually the case when you do not immediately remove anything that should not belong in that space. Remember to always keep away non-laundry related items out of the laundry room. Doing so helps prevent your freshly washed clothes from getting soiled and contaminated, and also makes it easier for you to actually perform different laundry tasks.

Streamline your laundry products

You might be surprised to know the exact number of products you actually need to do the laundry: Not that many. Choose a single detergent that can clean all types of fabrics instead of using different specialty products for different fabric needs. Try adding baking soda to the washer to give your detergent that extra boost; white vinegar can help soften your washed clothes, so that you can do away with using dryer sheets or fabric softeners.

Establish a spot for drying and folding

Not all laundered garments need to be added to the clothes dryer. Instead of subjecting your clothes to potential damage, let them air-dry on a retractable clothesline (wall mounted) or drying rack (freestanding). Designate a counter or table as your folding area, which you can also use when ironing clothes if you would rather not use an ironing board.

Set aside a place for every item

If your washer does not come with cabinets, consider having storage units/shelves installed above it to house your laundry products. This way, you keep the products organized and out of reach of your pets and children, who may accidentally get poisoned by these chemicals. You can also add more storage by bringing in wall baskets, over-the-door shelving, a rolling cart positioned between the dryer and washer, or a ledge or shelf at the back of your appliances. You can look for cheap baskets, boxes, and other containers to hold scissors, scrub brushes, clothespins, and other small items. You might also consider using a glass jar or basket for pocket items you that usually find before putting clothes in the washer; doing so helps make it easy for family members to look for and reclaim their missing items. You could likewise try assigning a basket for unpaired mittens and socks until you find their match. Remember to empty these baskets on a regular basis to really rein in clutter in the laundry room.

Sort things out

Consider purchasing individual dirty laundry hampers for each family member and each bathroom or linen closet. So whenever someone removes the washed clothes from the dryer, clothesline, or drying rack, he or she would simply fold the items before placing in the basket.

This is truly an effective way of teaching all family members the importance of looking after their own laundry to contribute to a clutter-free home.

Know what to keep in your laundry room

Basics: Here is a list of essential supplies you should have in the laundry room to ensure your tasks of taking care of clothes would be easy and enjoyable.

Bleach
Odor & stain removers
Detergent
Dryer sheets

Extra rags & towels – A stash of these items should be placed near your dryer and washer to help you in drying washed clothes flat as well as in mopping up spills and leaks.

Appliance instruction manuals – You can make the task of doing the laundry into less of a chore if you just make sure to have the instruction manuals for your washer, dryer, and other appliances close at hand. When you hear something banging or see something flickering in an alarming way, you can immediately solve the issue without having to leave the laundry room.

Sewing & ironing supplies – If the laundry room is where you normally mend torn garments and starch-spray and iron freshly laundered clothes, then it would make sense to keep your sewing and ironing tools in the same room.

Trash can – Your laundry room should have a trash can for catching all those scraps of packaging and dryer lint.

Cleaning supplies – Designate an area in the laundry room for the cleaning products you will be using for the space itself. You should not have to make trips to the bathroom or the kitchen if you need to use a broom or mop, some hand soap, or rolls of paper towels, especially when you already have plenty of tasks to deal with in the laundry room. It is also important to keep your cleaning supplies organized, so here are tips for you to follow to achieve that:

Put safety above everything else. Make sure to store all laundry room cleaning supplies out of your children's and pets' reach by placing them in a lockable closet or a high shelf. Otherwise, secure your storage units with drawer straps, cabinet straps, and other safety devices so that those tiny hands or paws are unable to play with hazardous chemicals.

Choose one spot in the laundry room to store your cleaning supplies. This will help you avoid having to track down that wood soap or toilet cleanser you need to use at the moment. It also helps to avoid stacking cans and bottles so deep that the only way you will be able to find a specific cleaning product is to burrow your way through all of them.

Make sure you have a portable caddy sitting near your cleaning supplies at all times. You will then simply place in the caddy whatever products you need to use, along with rags or towels, scrub brushes, and sponges.

See to it that your larger cleaning tools have a spot dedicated to storing them in your laundry room. Still, you might keep your steam mops, brooms, and vacuum cleaners in the basement, garage, or pantry. The important thing is that you are keeping these items next to one another so you have an easier time accessing them as needed.

Label everything as clearly as possible. While keeping your laundry room cleaning products in the exact bottles they came in when you bought them is great, there are times when you have to transfer them to other containers, such as spray bottles. In this situation, make sure to label them using label tapes and a permanent marker. For instance, this helps you and other family members avoid mistaking bleach for plain water.

Extras: Once you have the basic cleaning supplies all sorted out, you can now focus on choosing which laundry items to add to your list of must-haves in the laundry room. You may include the following:

Bins – for sorting the laundry into whites, lights, darks, towels, linens, and so on
Indoor clothesline or drying rack
Steamer
Iron and ironing board
Mesh bags – to fill with delicate items
Folding station – such as a shelf or a table
Clothespins

Try being creative with your laundry room storage
To succeed in decluttering the laundry room, you have to be able to utilize every inch of its available space. Take note of these tips when deciding on how to organize your laundry room:

Separate the space using curtains

If your laundry room does not have a door, but you really want it to be a separate space, try adding a partition with the help of curtains and a simple rod. This is an effective way of keeping your washer and dryer out of sight, even if the curtains do not necessarily offer any sound protection.

Put your appliances on a pedestal

One way of adding more storage space to your laundry room is fitting pedestal drawers below your washer and dryer units. Pedestal drawers raise your appliances above the ground, allowing you to access them more easily. Pick those that come with sectioned areas to better optimize the space and easily fit in your laundry supplies.

Utilize the back of doors

The back of your laundry room door offers a valuable spot for you to store various items. Find storage solutions that you would have used in your closets, such as a shoe storage unit that you simply hang over the door. You might also want to attach simple hooks on the door to provide extra space for hanging laundry bags or special hangers for air-drying your delicates.

Fill unused corners with shelving

They are easy to overlook in the laundry room, but those unused corners provide the right spots for extra shelving storage solutions. Try wall shelf options that you can easily fit into any space and that would be great for organizing your detergent and other laundry items.

Contain supplies in baskets

Optimize your shelves by adding storage containers like jars and baskets, which you can fill with your laundry supplies as well as use to give your laundry room some visual appeal without compromising on space. You could make use of old candy jars, vases, or apothecary jars to put your vintage items collection on display.

Chapter 7
Strategy 2: The Big Purge

Getting rid of stuff you no longer want in your home can be an overwhelming task, especially when you find yourself unable to decide right away whether you would hold onto certain items or give them up already. Fortunately, you have the following steps to guide you in carrying out the big purge around your house:

Setting goals
It is important to make a concrete plan on how you will go about decluttering your home in one big purge. Begin by:

Creating a map of all rooms in your home, as well as those clutter zones you plan on dealing with.

Grading each space in your home according to how cluttered it is. You might grade on a one to three scale, with one being the least cluttered and an especially disorganized room being given a three. Doing so enables you to make good use of your time.

Identifying your reasons for decluttering your home and how you believe it will improve your life. Doing so will motivate you into working past the difficulties of going through your stuff, figuring out which to keep and to toss, coming to terms with a sense of loss and other emotions, and getting your family members to cooperate in achieving your decluttering goals.

Visualizing how you would want your home to appear once you are done with your decluttering project. Really think about what every room, space, and corner in your house should look and feel like to you, your family, and to other people who enter your house.

Considering your lifestyle when decluttering your home. If you have little kids still running around the house, it would not be reasonable to try turning your living room into a fancy space where coffee table books are expected to stay perfectly undisturbed on the coffee table, which should not have any marks of chubby little hands pressing on them. It is important to think positive and dream big, but it is just as important to be realistic and rational with your visions of decluttering success.

Getting decluttering inspirations from Pinterest and other resources. This will help you figure out your decorating style, plan your organization strategies, feel even more motivated to tackle the mess in your home, and get the job done faster.

Thinking about making a decluttering vision board. You can glue pictures and words cut out of magazines onto a poster board. You might also try creating a collage with the help of digital apps. The important thing is to provide yourself a visual aid that represents your goals and that you will frequently see on a wall or on your phone. This way, you are constantly reminded, motivated, and focused on your desire to create a mess-free and organized home.

Preparing for your purging project

Get everything ready several days prior to the day you want to carry out the big purge in your home. Consider scheduling the purge during a weekend when there are no visitors, no lessons, no activities, and no games to distract you from your task. Gather your decluttering team, which includes your spouse, children, and other helpers. Making sure all family members are involved helps to encourage them to commit themselves to keeping your home uncluttered after all the hard work they have done.

It may be easy to go back to old bad habits that result in creating clutter, but it becomes difficult when you know you have exerted so much time and energy in getting rid of all that mess. If you have young kids, consider having them looked after by friends or relatives. If you have animals, try arranging for a pet sitter. You might want to prepare meals ahead of time so that you can truly focus on decluttering your home. It also helps to stock up on bottled water and granola bars to give to your team of helpers whenever they need an energy boost.

Establishing a sorting system

You need your sorting system to determine what you will do with each item you come across with as you walk through all spaces and rooms in your home. You may have a sorting method of your own, or you can follow the often-used three-box method, which encourages you to decide immediately on what to do with each item. The latter truly helps you avoid having to deal with more clutter than what you had in the beginning.

Get three storage bins or boxes and label as “Keep”, “Toss”, and “Store.

The “Keep” box is where you put those items you want to keep and give a new home. Ideally, your “Keep” items should be stored and organized inside a drawer or container. Empty this box once you are done with decluttering a space.

The “Toss” box is where you place and store those items that you want to either sell or donate. In the meantime, place this box in your transporting vehicle or temporarily store in your attic or garage. You should empty the “Toss” box once you have completely decluttered a space.
The “Store” box should be emptied into your storage units once you are done working on a space. Remember to label this box before placing tidily in your designated storage area.

Identifying the things you need to get rid of in the living area

DVDs & VHS tapes: You need to give up your never-watched old, scratched up tapes and discs if you tend to mostly watch movies on Hulu or Netflix.

DVD players & VCRs: If you do not use DVDs and tapes anymore, then you surely have no need for DVD players, VHS tape rewinders, and VCRs. As long as they are in good working condition, you can sell them online, donate them to people who still watch movies on DVD and tape, or dispose of them responsibly.

Random technology: Let go of random technology bits like cords and remotes that you no longer use. One way to know you may never use a particular item again is if you could not even figure out what it is. Give these items to someone who could use them or have them listed online.

Board games: A card deck would be useless if you do not have the ace, and a chess set is no fun if you lost the queen. Donate or sell all games that have certain pieces missing.

Children's toys: It is high time you dispose or donate your kids' old toys if they have already outgrown these things. If your kids are still young enough to play with their toys, but you can no longer take another day of tripping over their stuff, you can corral and organize a specific area for them to keep their toys in. Remember to let go of toys that have broken parts or that come in multiples.

Old newspaper & magazines: You may own stacks of old magazine issues lying in almost every corner of the living room. Ditch those that do not have any sentimental or historical value.

Knowing which stuff should not stay in your dining room and kitchen

Menus & receipts: Keep important documents in a filing cabinet near your desktop computer. Meanwhile, recycle or dispose of those that do not have any value. Snap pictures of your family's favorite takeout menus, then save on your phone to reduce or get rid of paper clutter in your dining room or kitchen. If you would rather hold on to the menus, make sure to arrange them in a file, dedicating a file holder to keep them organized on the kitchen counter. If they still cause a mess on the counter or in the drawers, it only means the method is not effective and that you should definitely digitize and eliminate them altogether.

Condiments and napkins from fast food restaurants: Letting go of things also means not throwing them out yet, using them all up for as long as they last instead, and as a result not adding to the waste already existing in the environment. This applies to your condiments (pack in lunches and use up during dinner until gone) and fast food napkins (place in a napkin holder and go through them within one to two weeks).

Duplicate kitchen essentials: You will know you literally have too much on your plate when you find yourself staring at six food scales, four cheese graters, and three salad spinners. Decide on which items are used regularly and should be kept, then ditch everything else that never make it to your list of usual tasks. Go through all your plastic containers and dispose of those with missing lids or that are permanently stained.

Unused stuff: It would be best to donate or sell your fondue set, even if it was given to you by your favorite aunt on your wedding day, if all it ever does in your kitchen is sit, collect dust, and contribute to visual clutter. Get rid of any old kitchen tool or equipment if it has broken parts and you never were able to get it fixed during the last one to two years.

Kiddie utensils & cups: Donate your grown kids' Disney utensils from the last two decades to Goodwill to free up additional space in your kitchen. Just make sure they are still in good condition so that other kids could use them.

Old party supplies: Birthday candles usually end up being mashed underneath other items inside the kitchen drawer. Get rid of clutter and make more space in your drawers by using them, along with forgotten extra party plates and napkins.

Excess dishes & cups: It may not hurt that you have more than enough kitchenware to use if additional guests come to your party, but you should treat anything unused in an entire year as excesses. If your home is just about to burst at the seams from all the party plates you have accumulated through the years, it may be wise to return said items to their owners. If this is not possible, you can donate those pieces that are still in good condition and dispose of those that are not.

Plastic bags: It is great to have a supply of plastic bags in the kitchen, ready to use as needed, but not if they end up taking up precious space and causing clutter because you do not actually use them up. If your local recycling center does not welcome plastic bags, you can dispose of your extra supply responsibly by offering it to grocery stores that are willing to recycle them.

Clearing the bedroom of the following items

Bedside table knickknacks: The only things you really need on a bedside table are a lamp, a notepad, a pen, and a charging dock. Adding anything else only ends up cluttering the tabletop, so either throw them out or move them to another part of your house. Search through the drawers to find other things you need to get rid of as well, especially if you know you have been stuffing odds and ends in there for a year or so. Fill the drawers only with essential bedtime items like your reading glasses, phone charger, medications, sleep mask, and flashlight.

Worn out/extra bedding: Each member of your family actually needs just two to three sets of sheets for the bed. This means you will need to think over your bedding inventory if you have too many extras crowding your linen closet. Check out local charities that would be willing to accept your in-good-condition bedding if you donated them; otherwise, give them away to animal shelters.

Mangled/broken hangers: Hangers that cannot be used in hanging clothes should be thrown out of the house. Quickly dispose of mangled, warped, or cracked hangers.

Plates & cups: If you are wondering why you have a growing number of cups littering your bedside week after week, you definitely need to clear them all out of the bedroom and bring them back to the kitchen. Avoid going through the cup-clutter stint all over again by dedicating a water cup for use during nighttime. Prevent any spills by opting for a water bottle or a cup that has a lid.

Deflated pillows: You can have too many pillows in your bedroom, especially those deflated ones that look worn out and never really do a good job of helping you go to sleep. Throw them out and replace with new durable pillows (assign two pillows per family member). This tip also applies to your extra throw pillows.

Eliminating these things from the bathroom

Hotel soaps: While there is something almost sacred about swiping soaps from hotels when you are traveling, the same cannot be said about your stolen stash getting mashed into drawers and making a mess on top of the bathroom counter. Consider moving them to a guest bathroom, provided they are organized tidily and are useful in the space. Otherwise, you and your bathrooms will be better off without them. Try donating your hotel soaps to local homeless shelters, which residents in need will surely appreciate and use.

Towels in bad condition: Instead of insisting on having five sets of bath towels for each family member, keep it down to three sets per person and donate the extra towels to your local charity. Just wash them first to ensure they are thoroughly clean and free from stains and the smell of mildew. Towels that look like they are beyond repair still have their use in animal shelters, where they will be used in cleaning up after the animals.

Multiple grooming tools: You really only need one each of grooming tools, which include your toothbrush, hairbrush, beard trimmer, razor, tweezers, eyelash curler, straightening iron, and hair dryer. You might need a duplicate for each of these tools so you will have one to use at home and another while traveling, but anything more than that is just inviting more clutter into your home. For sanitary reasons, you should not pass on your grooming supplies to other people, but you might be able to donate or sell your still-working hair dryer. Dispose or recycle all other extra hair appliances.

Expired medications: You do not need those expired medical supplies sitting in your drawers, so throw them out of the house. If you have old wheelchairs, crutches, or other medical devices lying around the house, donate them to a local hospital or charity so people who need them can use them.

Unused moisturizers: Ditch those bottles of moisturizers that only got used once. You probably hated their smell, or did not find them moisturizing enough. But whatever your reason for not using them, it is important that you remove them from the bathroom and get them into the nearest trash can or waste basket.

Banishing the following items from your garage

Extra tools: Store only those tools that are used regularly or on a seasonal basis. A branch trimmer, a hedge, and other tools that you do not often use and that you could easily rent or borrow can be sold or donated to add more space to your garage. Dispose of any item that is covered with rust or that is no longer in good working condition.

Forgotten building supplies: Quit pining for that day when you finally get to use those concrete blocks, bricks, or old pavers lying around and creating clutter in your garage. You will find that getting rid of these materials can be hard, as most curbside service companies are unable to take heavy debris. If you plan on disposing them, you could put up flyers in your neighborhood or bring them to a recycling center.

Busted sporting goods: Your garage does not deserve to be a dumping ground for flat basketballs, ruined shoulder pads, and snapped lacrosse sticks. Anything unusable should be taken away from the garage. If something is still in great condition, try donating it to a children's charity in your area or selling it online.

Leftover paint: In the proper conditions, you can store leftover paint in the garage for as long as ten to fifteen years. But temperature fluctuations in the garage can cause paint to dry up, never to be used again. If this is the case, it would be wise to responsibly dispose of leftover paint as well as paint-caked rollers and brushes.

Extra coolers: Camping supplies such as coolers usually gather and collect dust in the garage. Know that you do not need more than two of those. Keep a large cooler as well as a smaller, portable one and donate the rest (make sure they are functional and clean) to a Boy Scout or Girl Scout troop, whose members can use them during camping trips and parties. Busted coolers are not recyclable, which is why it is best to dispose of them; just make sure to remove the handles and lids first.

Excess pesticides and chemicals: Get rid of any diesel fuel, pesticides, and other excess chemicals sitting in your garage, especially when you have already traded in your vehicle the year before. Never burn, incinerate, pour down the drain, or dump into the grass these chemicals yourself; it is best to turn them over to the nearest hazardous waste center and let them handle the proper disposal of these substances.

Tackling these things straight out of the attic

Excess or damaged furniture: You probably have an old piece of furniture sitting in the attic, and the reason it was placed there could not be because you want to preserve its pristine condition for as long as possible. You might consider selling or donating your extra furniture pieces, but make sure they in good shape and are not damaged. Meanwhile, your dog-chewed recliner and torn bean bag chair should be immediately thrown away.

Unused appliances: Reclaim your storage area's valuable space by getting rid of your old washer, dryer, and other unused appliances.

Excess holiday décor: It is important to re-evaluate your holiday décor so you know whether or not you need to ditch certain items in favor of more storage space and less clutter. Unpack all the holiday boxes you have sitting in the attic, then decide on which items should stay and which should go (broken, cheap, etc.).

Old cardboard boxes: Recycle your old cardboard boxes as well as packaging materials. You may be surprised how doing so quickly results in your attic having more space and appearing less cluttered.

Multiple suitcases: One big suitcase is actually all it takes for you to be able to go on a long trip, and a duffel bag or a carry-on suitcase is enough to get you through a weekend trip. After you are done disposing of your extra luggage, keep the smaller bag inside the bigger one to optimize your attic's storage space.

Old baby items: Your daughter is now in college, so it is high time you let go of her baby stuff. Pass her old crib, strollers, and baby clothes on to someone else who needs these things. When giving away baby items, try searching for them in a database provided by the commission on Consumer Product Safety to give you an idea about whether or not they have been recalled. Never donate an old car seat–car seats can expire, making them less safe to use later on, especially if previously involved in accidents. Keep in mind that it is against the law to sell car seats that are expired, crashed, or recalled, which is why you need to ensure you are donating only those items that will not endanger the people receiving them.

Ridding the laundry room of these stuff

Torn clothes & mismatched socks: If you find it hard to determine where the other half of your favorite pair of socks is within the last six months, it might be time for you to believe it is gone. This means you need to toss all mate-less socks into the trash can. When it comes to torn clothes, decide whether you are going to repair them or throw them out immediately.

Expired cleaning products: Let go of all your old cleaning supplies, particularly the ones that are expired or that you simply never got around to using anymore, so you will have a newly cleared spot below the sink. Make sure to give your cleared cabinet interiors a good wiping down before filling once again with the items you want to keep.

Old keys: It would not be wise to just throw away your house keys and car keys, but consider throwing away that set of keys you have hanging on a hook without being used for the last five years. Before ditching them though, do ask your family if they have an idea on where to use those keys. Rule out possible matches within your house by trying the old keys on all doors, closets, and safes. Once you are sure the keys have no matches and that you already have in your possession all the accounted keys you need, you can finally toss them into the trash.

Extra detergent bottles: You may be keeping all those empty laundry detergent containers because you intend to reuse them sometime. Either take action on that intention right now, or have them recycled instead. You will always have more bottles to deal with for as long as you will be washing clothes.

Miscellaneous items: Besides providing you a space for cleaning your clothes, your laundry room may also be used for a host of other reasons that are totally unrelated to doing the laundry. You and your family probably use the space in storing coats and shoes as you walk into your house, or it may be where you keep your pet's food supply and other necessities handy. Make it a rule to let any item that gets used on a regular basis stay in the laundry room, but to throw out anything that just sits unused.

Chapter 8
Room-by-Room Decluttering vs. One Big Purge

Decluttering your entire house, even with the help of all of your family members, can be a daunting task. It becomes even more difficult when you have not decided yet whether to declutter using the room-by-room method or by going at it in one big purge.

Room-by-room decluttering involves working on a small space, then evaluating the result. If you are satisfied with how it turned out, you try working again, this time on another space or room in the house. The downside to this type of decluttering, however, is that it may take a long while before you observe any real progress. You may find it next to impossible to tackle on the attic, basement, and other clutter-prone areas of your home. You may find yourself not being able to finish organizing your photos or looking after your cherished objects.

Doing the big purge, on the other hand, involves getting all that clutter out of the house quickly so that you can attend to other aspects of your life. This type of decluttering gives you immediate results and frees you from the burden of maintaining stuff that no longer add value to your life. Purging your house in one go can also motivate you to declutter other areas in your life. But, this decluttering method requires that you have the mindset and determination to decide on what to do with your belongings at the drop of a hat.

This is why combining the two and achieving what can be considered the best of both worlds is often ideal. Decluttering room by room gives you a sense of accomplishment early on, while doing the big purge ensures that you immediately have more room and more space available while working, which provides you a better perspective when it comes to organizing and storing what is left after getting rid of the clutter.

Chapter 9
Putting Your Priorities in Perspective

In prioritizing your belongings and sentimental items in the process of decluttering your home, you need to ask yourself the following questions:

Would I want my family to have this when I'm gone?

Keep in mind that the stuff you own now, that you are probably proud of and happy about for having, will be a burden to the people who will inherit them. The truth is that being rich in life does not necessarily mean having acquired a huge number of possessions; it can mean living with the people you love in a home that is free from clutter and bad memories.

What are the things I need at this point of my life?

Your priority in life is probably making sure your family's needs are regularly met. But if you choose to hold onto specific sentimental items, which force you to fixate on things of the past, you end up having less focus on the things that are important to you at present.

Which belongings do I keep?

Instead of asking yourself which stuff you should give up, try asking yourself which things would you want to hold onto. Gather those for-keeps items in one place where you can easily spot them. This way, you are constantly reminded that you have the best things in your possession, and it becomes easier for you to let go of all the other stuff.

Am I ready to give up my purpose and passion in exchange for my belongings?

Remind yourself of the price you have to pay in order to keep certain belongings around. There are times when you are better off feeling the pain of letting go of sentimental items than feeling weighed down from keeping them around.

Putting Excess Clutter to Good Use

It's great that you have finally cleared the mess out of your home, but now you have to know what to do with all the excess clutter. Below are ideas on how to put them to good use instead of sending them to the landfill.

Put them up for sale

Consider selling your unwanted but still usable items through your phone. You can post on online community pages or on your social media by typing "Buy/Sell" into the search engine of your Facebook account. You are bound to easily find a marketplace within your local community in this manner. If the thought of selling a lot of items overwhelms you, just think about how this task is way better than sending in-good-condition belongings to the dump just because you no longer liked them.

If you have books to sell, check out BookScouter.com, which can help you search for online book buyers who are willing to pay the highest prices. You could also have your books listed on Half.com, a site currently owned and operated by eBay. You could likewise try going to stores that carry used books and have the business owners go through your collection so they could buy it from you if they like what they see.

If your excess clothes are still in good condition, try selling the best ones to consignment stores or through eBay. Divide the remaining garments into lots before posting an ad in the local classifieds or on Craigslist. Whatever clothing you have left can then be put up for sale in a yard sale. If you have vintage clothes just gathering dust in the attic, consider selling it on Etsy.com.

If your excess clutter includes antiques, collectibles, and furniture of exceptional quality, you could sell those items at an auction or on consignment. Have your good-quality pieces listed in your local newspaper's classifieds or on Craigslist. Sell the remaining pieces at your yard sale or through a dealer that specializes in antiques and collectibles.

You could sell your sports equipment, making sure they are lightly used, to sports shops that offer used goods. You may also post fliers or sell what remains through local classified ads, Craigslist, or pawnshops.

Sell your newer electronics through the classifieds, Craigslist, or eBay. If you have older but usable electronic items as well, try selling them through a yard sale, Craigslist, or a classified ad. Even broken or obsolete electronic items may be sold through eBay or recycled through Best Buy.

You can sell your newer releases of CDs, DVDs, and video games at GameStop, on eBay, on Craigslist, or through local classified ads. You can also have them sold through sites that purchase used CDs, DVDs, and video games, like SecondSpin.com, or get them listed on Half.com.

Sell your in-demand housewares on eBay, through Craigslist, through the classifieds, or on consignment. Whatever is left can then be sold at your garage sale.

If your excess clutter includes working appliances, you have an opportunity to make money off them. Get them listed in the local newspaper or on Craigslist. Broken appliances, on the other hand, can be listed on eBay or sold for scrap through the recycling center. You could also donate old appliances that still work to local thrift stores or charities.

After having your good-quality pieces of jewelry as well as your antiques appraised, you can sell them to a jewelry store, through eBay, at auctions, or to a dealer. Lesser jewelry pieces may still be sold through eBay or on consignment, while junk jewelry may be sold for scrap value to jewelry stores. You could also try selling your low-end costume pieces at a yard sale.

Sell your used musical instruments as well as audio equipment through Reverb.com or by contacting band directors that work with high schools and middle schools. Alternatively, you can advertise through classified ads or on Craigslist to get the word out that you are selling used musical instruments. If all else fails, you could try selling them to pawnshops or music shops instead.

Give them to people who need or want them
Start by figuring out the things will you be selling (through a garage sale or online) and what things will you be giving away. If you are pressed for time or would really help your local community, consider donating your stuff instead of selling them. Either way, you give other people an opportunity to benefit from the stuff you gave up as well as help in keeping your trash from finding its way to a landfill. As soon as you have determined which pieces will be donated, see to it that every item is in good condition, functional, and thoroughly cleaned.

Furniture, kitchen supplies, toys, bedding, and clothing

Shelters: You can give clothing, bedding, and other unwanted household items to support agencies like local shelters so that you can take part in helping unfortunate individuals start anew in life. Try checking the local directory for particular organizations you could donate your stuff to.

Thrift stores & non-profit shops: Goodwill, Salvation Army, and other charities could use the stuff you no longer need. You could also donate to smaller non-profit organizations with storefronts that will sell your items for a profit, which goes back to the community. These agencies partner with local shelter in ensuring that proper clothing and other supplies find their way to people who actually need them.

Consignment stores: Although they specialize in vintage garments, consignment stores welcome designer items as well as rarely worn clothing. They will offer you money or a discount in return for having them put your stuff up for sale. Remember that these stores will either pay you upfront with cash or give you payment only once your items are sold.

Office supplies, books, and magazines

Libraries & literacy organizations: The local public library may not welcome your used books, but they might request you to donate said books to a literacy group in your community, one that may be part of the library services. Your donation may also end up being put to good use by a poorly funded or ill-equipped local library in a rural area. Just ask the local librarian for guidance in searching for groups and organizations that badly need your used books, magazines, and other reading materials.

Daycare centers & schools: While your child may go to a well-equipped school, there are many schools, and even daycare centers that can only provide slightly used books to students. Your books and magazines will be of great help to these places.

Bookstores selling used books: There are bookstores that are willing to receive your slightly used books and news magazines, trading them for books or cash.

Shelters & support services: These places usually serve as resources for both the local neighborhood and their residents through their in-house libraries. A lot of people cannot access books in the library for lack of a permanent address, which is why their sole resource for reading materials is a shelter bookshelf. Try calling local nonprofit support groups to know what they need and which books and magazines you will be donating.

Office supplies: Any nonprofit organization will find your boxes of unused copy paper and barely used crayons useful. Your extra school supplies will find good homes in family shelters, daycare centers, schools, and community centers.

Computers and electronic equipment

Community centers & schools: Local community centers and schools usually welcome used computer equipment for use by residents, local students, or local families.

Shelters & non-profit agencies: These places specialize in making sure that families starting anew are able to set up a household, which is why they will welcome your computer, television set, or stereo.

Non-profit shops & thrift stores: Take your working electronics equipment and computers to these places, which will gladly accept your donations. Do not forget to check that your stuff do work and make sure you have deleted all of your personal information from the hard drives.

Have them repaired

Once an object is broken, it tends to lose its functional value. The thing is, there are many things that you can easily repair, requiring only a new part and a little effort. Having your broken items repaired allows you to save the money you would have spent buying new ones to replace them. Rather than throwing any broken object out of your home and into a landfill, try having it repaired. If this fails, you can always keep on using it, sell it, or donate it.

Bring them to the recycling center

If you live in an area where public recycling services are available, whether in the form of a processing center that is centralized and accepts things you drop off, or as a curbside pickup service, then you have no reason to avoid recycling your excess clutter. Research on what the local recycling center allows, keeping in mind that most welcome batteries, light bulbs, metal, glass, paper, cardboard, and plastic jugs. Recycling centers also usually have a processing station dedicated to electronic items such as TV sets, stereo equipment, and video recording equipment, as well as cables, remotes, and other electronic accessories.

Find ways to repurpose them

If it is not possible for you to recycle, donate, or sell your excess clutter, try finding ways to repurpose your excess clutter. Consider:

Using old t-shirts as rags for washing the car
Sewing your family members' old garments together to create a memory quilt
Turning your spouse's old shirts into pillowcases
Using toilet paper rolls as cords and cables organizer
Making a coin bank out of a plastic container
Using old jeans as draft stoppers
Making a knife block out of a box filled with wooden skewers
Creating a serving tray out of an old picture frame
Making your puppy a chew toy by tying up an old tennis ball in an old sock
Making a medicine cabinet out of your old suitcase
Turning old jeans into sturdy potholders
Making a watering can out of an empty laundry detergent bottle
Turning old tea cups into succulent pots

Have your done-for stuff hauled out by a dumpster

Renting a dumpster lets you get rid of a large number of need-to-go items after decluttering in a convenient and affordable way. Simply follow these steps:

Call the dumpster rental service

Ask for a quote free of charge. You will need to provide information about the volume and type of debris you are getting rid of.

Ask for upfront pricing

This should include your rental period, pickup, disposal, and delivery. The dumpster rental service team will discuss with you the items you can place in the dumpster so that you can effectively declutter.

Schedule your preferred date of delivery

The dumpster rental company should promptly deliver the container you need to start working. Make sure to discuss how the delivery process goes to avoid any drop off mishaps.

Call the dumpster rental company for pickup

Give them another call the moment you are done filling up your dumpster. The company will then set a date and time for picking it up.

Chapter 10
Frequently Asked Questions You Need to Address

Now that you have truly embraced decluttering as a way of living your life with more freedom, less stress, less worry, and more joy, it is important that you regularly check yourself, your home, and your possessions to avoid finding yourself back in the messy way of life you spent so much time and effort on to break free from.

Remember to always ask yourself these questions when handling an item:
Does my life derive great benefits when I use such item on a daily, weekly, or monthly basis?

Do I own something that I use to perform a certain task and that I can also use for other purposes?

Is this object a representation of my special relationship with an important person in my life?

Does this object depict a life-changing experience I once went through in the past?

Do I experience an immense feeling of happiness, contentment, or excitement when I see or use this item?

Do I find this object so beautiful that my emotions are stirred each time I set my sights on it?

Does this item spark feelings of curiosity and wonder in me?

Does this object serve as a balm to my spirit in ways that cannot be explained with words?

Do I love this item so much that I want to use it as much as I can, day in and day out?

Do I love using this object so much that I find myself looking for ways to use it in different tasks or in different aspects of my life?

Is this item in my possession because it serves a purpose or gives me feelings of joy and adventure, and not because people expect me to own such item?

Do I feel like a competent, confident, and brilliant individual whenever I have this item on or with me?

Do I see myself buying this item again, even if ends up costing twice as much?

Would I find it in my heart to get this item repaired no matter what if it gets broken or damaged?

Is this item something I have used on a fairly regular basis during the past year?

Do I see myself using this object again for the next twelve months, and would I still feel happy, contented, or excited each time?

Would I want to bring this object with me if I moved to another place?

Conclusion

I hope this book was able to help you realize that decluttering is a project you can take on with the help of your family in order to make your dream of living in a clean and happy home come true.

The next step is to avoid allowing clutter to rule over your home and your life ever again. Remember to do little bits of decluttering on a daily basis and to let go of the thrill of buying something just because.

Printed in Great Britain
by Amazon

85088096R00045